HAUNTED THEATERS

Barbara Smith

GHOST
HOUSE

Ghost House Books

© 2002 by Barbara Smith and Ghost House Books
First printed in 2002 10 9 8 7 6 5 4 3 2 1
Printed in Canada

The Publisher: Ghost House Books
Distributed by Lone Pine Publishing
10145 – 81 Avenue
Edmonton, AB T6E 1W9
Canada

Website: http://www.ghostbooks.net

National Library of Canada Cataloguing in Publication Data
Smith, Barbara, 1947-
    Haunted theaters

    ISBN 1-894877-04-7

    1. Ghosts. 2. Haunted places. 3. Theaters. I. Title.
BF1461.S578 2002   33.1'22   C2002-910330-4

Editorial Director: Nancy Foulds
Project Editor: Shelagh Kubish
Editorial: Shelagh Kubish, Chris Wangler
Illustrations Coordinator: Carol Woo
Production Coordinator: Jennifer Fafard
Cover Design: Rod Michalchuk
Layout & Production: Jeff Fedorkiw
Photo Credits: The photographs in the book are reproduced with the generous permission of their owners: © Bill Fink Communications (p.17, p.19, chapter introductions); Bird Cage Theatre (p.27); Elgin and Winter Garden Theatres (p.69); J.T. Smith (p.88); David A. Tucker and the Pasadena Playhouse archives (p.99); Glenbow Archives, Calgary, Alberta, Canada, #NA-5464-1 (p.109); Bagdad Theatre (p.125); Walnut Street Theatre (p.137); Barbara Smith (p.183); Royal Alexandra Theatre (p.188); Grand Theatre, London, Ontario (p.210).

We acknowledge the financial support of the Government of Canada through the Book Publishing Industry Development Program (BPIDP) for our publishing activities.

PC: P6

DEDICATION

*This book is dedicated to the memory of my parents who,
in their very different ways,
shared with me their love of the theatre.*

PROGRAM

~

ACKNOWLEDGMENTS

I AM AN EXPERT ON NEITHER THE THEATER NOR THE paranormal, but merely a storyteller with a special love of the theater—stage and screen—who also happens to be fascinated by the phenomenon of ghosts. I wish, therefore, to acknowledge a great debt of gratitude to researchers who have gone before me in both fields.

My sincere thanks to the people identified within all the stories in this book. They all gave generously of their time in sharing their knowledge and experiences with me.

In addition, it would have been impossible for me to have written this book without the generous support of the following people: Randy Alldread with the Royal Alexandra Theatre in Toronto, Ontario; Ellen Bailey with the Pasadena Playhouse in Pasadena, California; Steve Bartlett of Chatham, Ontario; W. Ritchie Benedict, Calgary, Alberta; Laurel Cook, Edmonton, Alberta; Bill Fink, Houghton, Michigan; Audrey Frair, Calumet, Michigan; David Hastings, Victoria Theatre, Dayton, Ohio; Dick Hazzard, Executive Director of the Calumet Theatre, Calumet, Michigan; Janet Hewlett-Davies, Little Theatre Rep, Brighton, England; Leslie Holth, Pumphouse Theatres in Calgary, Alberta; Brent Hyams, Senior Marketing Manager with the Ryman Auditorium, Nashville, Tennessee; Laura Januzzi, Victoria Theatre, Dayton, Ohio; Sheila Johnston, Grand Theatre in London, Ontario; Lynne Kendrick, International Theatre Institute, London, England; Dr. Felicia Londre; Heather MacKenzie, Charlottetown, Prince Edward Island; Margaret and Marc Marra, Red Deer, Alberta; Vilda Poole, Prince Albert, Saskatchewan; Dee

Rodriguez, San Antonio, Texas; Isabel Rodriguez, Majestic Theatre, San Antonio, Texas; J.T. Smith, Sanibel, Florida; Dr. Vincent Scasselliti, Kansas City, Missouri; Reg. A. (Dutch) Thompson, Charlottetown, Prince Edward Island; Dr. Bill Worley, Kansas City, Missouri; The Glenbow Museum and Archives, Calgary, Alberta; Susan Mattingly, Lyric Theatre, Blacksburg, Virginia. I thank you all for your friendly support and contributions to my work.

Although we have never met, Bonnie Robbins of Brandon, Manitoba, adopted this project as though it were her own. Thank you, Bonnie, for all the leads you sent my way and for your many cheery notes.

I also want to thank the people who are closest to me in my day-to-day life. My dear friend and fellow ghost story author, Jo-Anne Christensen, without whom no day would be complete! My "first-run" editor and endlessly supportive advisor and close friend, Dr. Barrie Robinson. Thank you, Barrie, for your more than considerable contribution to this book. I have so appreciated your efforts and support. And, of course, thanks always to Bob, Debbie and Robyn.

Finally, thank you to all the people at Ghost House Books. Please know that I truly admire and appreciate your many and varied talents. Special thanks to Shane Kennedy, Nancy Foulds, Shelagh Kubish, Chris Wangler and Jeff Fedorkiw.

INTRODUCTION

WHILE RESEARCHING MY PREVIOUS GHOST STORY books, I was struck by how many theaters are haunted. Having grown up attending the standard Saturday afternoon movies and also various live stage performances, I was especially intrigued by this haunting phenomenon. Not surprisingly, collecting and writing the stories for this book became an irresistible project for me, a perfect convergence of lifelong passions.

Theaters, and the people involved with them, are unique entities in our society. To make a play or a movie effective, one group of people—the actors—agree to pretend that they are someone other than who they really are. They do this in order to entertain the other equally important group of people—the audience—who agree to temporarily suspend their disbelief. Without these unspoken agreements, there could be no theater; with these agreements, all theaters become magic places where time shifts and identity is transformed.

Theaters built today are more sparsely and economically designed than they were in the early 1900s when theater architecture and interior decoration were at least as, and often more, dramatic and extravagant as any production being presented. Lush fabrics with rich, dark colors accented lavish interiors. Elaborate (and expensive!) artwork adorned walls and ceilings, and chandeliers abounded. From the moment patrons purchased their admission tickets, they were transported to a world much more exotic than the one they had stepped from.

Given these opulent surroundings, it's not surprising

that theater-goers dressed in their finest clothes. Anything else would have seemed disrespectful in such an elegant setting. Uniformed employees wearing spotlessly clean white gloves treated every member of the audience with utmost courtesy. Just going to the theater was itself an enchanting experience; the actual entertainment was sometimes incidental. (One mustn't glamorize the "good old days" too much, though. Along with this splendor, many theaters posted signs advising the less sensitive members of the crowd that "Spitting on the floor is prohibited by law.") Given all the financial, physical, intellectual and emotional investments people make for theaters, it's no wonder that so many of them are haunted.

Collecting and writing these ghost stories has been a marvelous adventure. I hope you enjoy reading them. My warmest thanks to my publisher, Shane Kennedy, for supporting this project, which has meant so much to me for so many years.

GLOSSARY OF THEATER TERMS

*M*ANY PHRASES USED IN THEATERS, AND BY THEATER people, have supernatural connotations. For instance, during a day (or days) when no show is playing at a venue, a rather eerie term is used: the theater is said to be "dark." This term is used although the stage is never left in complete darkness—illumination created by a perpetually illuminated "ghost light" prevents darkness from ever fully descending. A ghost light is usually a single light bulb, sitting on top of a tripod and connected by an electrical cord to the nearest power outlet. Pragmatic thespians (a fancy word for actors) explain that the ghost light is needed so that the first person into the auditorium can see well enough to turn on the other lights. It's tough to argue with the practical logic behind such reasoning. Folks with a slightly more whimsical bent say the fixture is called a ghost light because it stands alone, like a ghostly sentinel. I've also been told that the ghost light is always left on out of consideration for the theater's resident ghosts. No doubt different opinions are favored in different theaters.

For clarity, a few of the many terms associated with theaters are defined here, in alphabetical order.

backstage: any part of the area behind the stage including the wings (see definition), workshops, storerooms and dressing rooms.

burlesque: came to be associated with risqué entertainment, but in Victorian England it began as musical entertainment.

flies: the area high above the stage (usually hidden from the audience's view), from which scenery, lighting and other equipment necessary to produce a show can be suspended.

fly gallery: a platform located well above floor level and toward the backstage area; scenery can also be rigged from this platform.

flyman: a stagehand who maneuvers riggings for scenery and curtains.

FOH: an abbreviation for the term "front of the house," which refers to both the name of the department within the theater that looks after security, the lobby and the box office, as well as to those areas themselves. The term is also used to describe the area on the audience's side of the curtain—or anything that occurs there.

gaffer: the stage crew's department head or foreman.

gallery *or* **the gods:** either the highest balcony or the occupants of that space (sometimes a ghost!).

ghost light: a single bulb atop a tripod left illuminated on the stage when the rest of the theater is dark.

ghost walks: an old expression used to indicate that the theater company's manager is delivering the weekly pay.

green room: the theater's traditional waiting or reception room. It is located near the stage and serves as a meeting place for guests or a place where actors can spend free time. Tradition dictates that the green room is never painted green. According to George Burns' book, *All My Best Friends,* the name green room originated in vaudeville days when playwright Edward Albee had billiard and pool tables added to staff lounges so that the performers could while away their leisure hours hunched over the green felt table coverings.

grip: a stagehand who helps the carpenter move scenery.

house: used to describe both the audience attending a performance and the auditorium in which that audience is seated; within ghostly theater lore, there are many haunted houses.

house lights: the lights that illuminate the auditorium.

legitimate theater: has come to mean live, as opposed to taped, entertainment. Historically, any production relying on a musical-comedy vaudeville show was not considered to be "legitimate theater."

prop: an object that the actors use, manipulate and/or move to help get the meaning of the performance across to the audience. The word used was originally "property," but with common usage it was shortened and has become a word in its own right.

proscenium arch: an arch that separates the stage from the auditorium and helps to frame the performance. Historically, these arches have been ornate works of art. Most modern theaters have dispensed with this architectural feature.

stage manager: the person in charge of all performances after final dress rehearsals are completed; in charge of the stage crew (those working on creating the stage setting) and responsible for ensuring that all goes smoothly both on the stage and backstage during a performance. Before the position of director was developed in the 20th century, the stage manager was also often in charge of rehearsals. He (in that era the position was overwhelmingly held by men) was usually helped by an assistant stage manager who sometimes also acted or worked as a dialogue prompter for actors who momentarily forgot their lines.

stage left *or* **stage right:** directions given according to the performers' left or right when they are facing the audience.

state theater/re: a term used in the United States; an honorary title indicating acknowledgment of the theater's exceptional quality.

theatre *or* **theater:** this word can be spelled (correctly!) either way. In this book, for consistency, we have chosen to use the "er" suffix except when the name of the venue uses the spelling "theatre."

Theatre Royal: Many of Britain's theaters bear the title "Theatre Royal," which indicates they have received royal approval. In order to avoid confusion, each Theatre Royal identifies itself by geographical location (for example, Drury Lane Theatre Royal).

vaudeville: a corruption of the name of the town in France where the satirical musical comedy style began.

vomitoria *or* **vomitory:** as used in the theater, these words have meanings not nearly as gruesome as you might first imagine. The main doors to the seating area can be referred to as the vomitoria. In English theater, the vomitory is the entrance rather than the actual doors. Variations on this word (including the diminutive "vom") generally refer to ways of leaving or entering the stage and/or auditorium; that is, patrons or actors are disgorged through these areas. (The term has its roots in a Latin word meaning to "throw up" or "throw forth.")

wings: the areas just off the stage on either side of the main acting space. The term is also used to refer to the strategically arranged screens that obscure these areas from the audience's view.

~

STAGE PRESENCE

Modjeska's Manifestation

Helena Modjeska. Not exactly a household name today—unless your household happens to be interested in theatrical history or located in Calumet, on Michigan's Upper Peninsula. In either of those cases, you would know that Madame Modjeska was an internationally famous actress who specialized in Shakespearean roles. She died in 1909, at the age of 69, and has been haunting the Calumet Theatre for most of the years since her death.

Modjeska first played at the Calumet in 1900 when she was 60 years old. She returned twice before her death. "She did love coming here," a theater employee said.

Unlike some theaters, where the resident spirit is accepted or tolerated at best, Madame Modjeska's presence in Calumet is embraced by everyone associated with the magnificent place. Volunteer archivist Audrey Frair informed me, "We have a large portrait of Modjeska hanging at the back of the theater."

Nick Healy, a reporter with the *Daily Mining Gazette*, wrote, "They say the spirit of Helena Modjeska roams the catwalk above the stage, toils in dressing rooms and looms in a dark, claustrophobic hallway running behind the seats in the now-closed second balcony."

Lorraine Vorase, who often acted as a tour guide for the theater, emphatically told a reporter, "Our ghost is very real to us."

Actress Adysse Lane firmly believed that she was saved from public and professional humiliation by Helena Modjeska's ghost. The incident of ghostly intervention

The ghost of a Shakespearean actress haunts the Calumet Theatre in Michigan.

occurred during the summer of 1958. Lane was playing Kate in *The Taming of the Shrew*. All had gone well during the performances. Nearing the end of the play, the role of Kate calls for a long and important soliloquy. On this particular night, a performer's worst nightmare came true for Adysse Lane. At that crucial point in the play, she forgot her lines. Her mind went blank.

Initially, and cleverly, Lane stalled for time with hand gestures that she hoped the audience would interpret as significant. Moments later, though, the truth was becoming obvious and Lane was beginning to panic. The nearly mortified actress suddenly felt her arm being lifted until her hand was pointing up toward a spot on the theater's balcony. There, impossibly, stood an image that Adysse Lane recognized immediately. It was Helena Modjeska. The image, appearing near a spotlight, was clearly visible from the stage. The long-deceased thespian mouthed the needed lines to the stricken actress and, in so doing, saved the play and Lane's pride.

Sometime after that evening, Adysse Lane described the ghostly figure she had seen as having "dark eyes and a pale complexion, Modjeska's face atop a fuzzy outline of a body." Even by the summer of 1965, when she had cause to reflect upon the encounter, Lane remembered it clearly. "Modjeska found me and saved me," the grateful actress stated.

There have been many reports of otherworldly activity since then. Audrey Frair explained that "recently, a lady who claims to be psychic encountered Modjeska and a whole bevy of figures approaching her in a narrow hallway. The lady was frightened and asked them in a loud voice to 'GO BACK.' They faded from view."

Modjeska's ghost is generally accepted as being friendly, although occasionally noisy. A few people associated with the theater feel there is a connection between the spirit's hijinks and the presence or absence of Madame Modjeska's portrait. Those folks maintain that the spirit becomes restless when, for whatever reason, the picture is temporarily taken down. It is usually at these times that people in the theater report feeling "the weight of her stare" but "look up and see nothing."

In 1959, Larry Carrico was working as the technical director for a troupe producing the play *A Streetcar Named Desire*. After the run, Carrico readily admitted to having been terrified when, on several different occasions, he felt an invisible presence brush past him on the stairway.

Other ghostly goings-on are typical of a haunted building. Employees who turn lights off and secure an area will return to find the lights on. The stage curtain, known to be drawn at night, will be open in the morning even though no one has been in the theater. A disembodied voice has been heard singing, but the source of the music could never be established. An employee, who for unreported reasons stayed the night in the theater, tried to sleep on the stage. He wasn't able to get much sleep because he kept hearing what sounded like heavy chunks of plaster falling.

Rick Rudden, a local reporter, also spent a night alone in the haunted theater. His reasons were straightforward—the stay would make a great story. Before evening fell on that fateful night in 1979, Rick interviewed Gloria Coello, at the time the theater's manager. A skeptic, Coello nonetheless related the employee's story of the noisy and sleepless night he'd experienced. Immediately after detailing the events, Coello was called away from her office. Moments later, Rudden was badly startled. "I distinctly heard a large piece of plaster fall to the floor," he wrote.

That evening, however, the loudest noise Rudden heard before he tried to catch some shut-eye was the

A rehearsal at the Calumet Theatre.

pounding of his own heart. He admitted that, for hours, he nervously prowled the dark and empty building. It wasn't until he lay down to sleep that he began to hear a series of phantom sounds: knocks that came from below the stage, doors that shook and "a long violent rattle." There was also a sound he was never able to identify but which he described as the sound of someone banging a large metal object against radiator pipes.

The Calumet Theatre may have been haunted for its entire 100-year history. The occasionally noisy, but often helpful, ghost of Madame Helena Modjeska has become an accepted and important part of the community's folklore.

SCENE II

Phantom Prom Queen

The theater was dark, save the ghost light.

Its single halogen orb cast a puddle of illumination upon the stage. Employee Dustin Wagner's footsteps echoed throughout the empty theater as he approached the light. Then, out of the darkness, a disembodied face suddenly appeared. The man's heart rate jolted to a new high, but only for a moment because the phantom face had only startled Dustin, not scared him. He'd worked at the Ventura Theatre in Ventura, California, for years and knew the place was haunted.

Dustin's friend and co-worker Nathan Beavers was used to "faces that pop out of the darkness. Then you turn on the lights and there's no one there." Dustin himself had seen "human shadows, different moving shadows."

Those partial specters are a complete mystery to theater employees. Yet the ghosts of Chester and Isabel are both recognized and understood. Chester worked—and died—at the theater more than 50 years ago. Although his death was officially declared an accident, many people now believe that Chester was murdered; that may be why he is not a pleasant entity.

"Chester's ghost doesn't like me," Nathan stated flatly. It could be that some of Nathan's jobs at the theater remind the ghost of the way the long-deceased man met his death. "Chester was installing or fixing the chandelier. I figure someone pulled the ladder out from under him, because why else would his spirit stay in the theater? There has to be a reason he's so angry. I get this feeling like I shouldn't be alone in certain places. Lately, I've been doing repair work on the place. Ever since I started doing that kind of thing, all of a sudden it's like I've been targeted."

While he was trying to clean one of the chandeliers in the building, Dustin had an especially distressing experience. "I was up on this old rickety ladder and reaching out to change a light bulb, but it kept getting farther and farther away. I kept stretching and reaching and then I thought, *wait a second—I should have grabbed it by now!* But whenever I went to reach for the bulb, it visibly moved away from my hand. I'm thinking this is just like a scene from a classic horror movie and I'm going to fall and decapitate myself on the bars of the chandelier. So I thought, *I'm going to outsmart this guy.* I crawled up higher, grabbed the chain of the chandelier, and pulled the whole fixture toward me."

Having won that particular battle with the angry phantom, Dustin hastily changed the bulb that had required his attention and then gratefully climbed down the ladder to the safety of the floor below.

Dustin added, "Chester's almost a poltergeist kind of ghost. Keys disappear and sometimes the chairs get moved and thrown about. It's *always* cold when he's there."

On another occasion, Dustin was waiting for other workers to join him in a remote corner of the theater. He said he "saw a light click on and tan pants and black shoes—like the kind I usually wear—going up a ladder, I thought, *okay, someone's already up there,* so I started to follow, but I noticed right away that the door to go up to the roof wasn't open! When I looked inside the door, no one was in there. I called out 'hello' and no one answered, so I said, 'Screw this—I'm not going in.' I felt like Chester wanted to get me alone."

Being with his friend Nathan may have given Dustin the confidence he needed to "chase a cold spot." Despite the possibility of safety in numbers, the anomaly came away the winner. Dustin "ended up getting thrown off the ground. It happened in the bar in the theater. I think that was Chester, too."

On February 7, 2000, Chester may have performed an amazing demonstration of supernatural strength. Dustin began, "We had a show that day. I moved the barricade that we use at punk shows to keep the kids off the stage and keep the band safe because the show that day didn't require it. Moving such a barricade was no easy job."

He continued, "These are huge wooden blocks. They're about 250 pounds each and they butt right up against the stage so you can walk right up. I can barely budge one of these things. I can pick it up by a side and I can slide it and drag it but that's all. I'm not a little guy. I weigh 230 pounds."

The scheduled show went on and all was well. The next day, the staff had to rearrange the set-up to prepare for a performance by a punk band. This meant removing the steps from in front of the stage and putting the barrier back in place. When the workers went to the spot where the barricade was stored, they were almost unable to believe their eyes. There, behind the stored barricade, was one of the enormous wooden steps.

There would have been almost unimaginable logistics involved in moving the massive wooden block of steps to that awkward location. In addition, Dustin knew for certain that absolutely no one, at least no living person, could have been in the theater overnight since he'd been the last one to leave after the performance. Moreover, just before he locked up, he observed that *all* the steps were right where they should have been—leading up to the stage.

What Dustin and two other workers found the next time they entered the theater spooked them all. "One of those giant stair blocks had been thrown behind the barricade. Not stacked like stairs or anything—just casually tossed, like it was a rag doll." Dustin is convinced that he knows who is responsible for the prank: "I totally think it was Chester."

No one is quite as sure which phantom of the Ventura Theatre was behind the next paranormal stunt, but it too was quite dramatic. The theater was hosting a "goth club" get-together. (Sociologist Dr. Barrie Robinson describes goths as "an offshoot of the punk movement, identified mainly for their fascination with the supernatural, mysticism and, for some, the occult…[They] have a penchant for black clothes, white makeup on their faces, black lipstick and black fingernails, thereby evoking images of the walking undead and a general sense of nihilism/despair.") Ventura Theatre employees decorated the place accordingly, even including a dummy of a ghostly angel with a skeleton face. Dustin explained, "The goths like that kind of stuff, so we were just trying to make them happy."

That thoughtfulness nearly had a disastrous outcome. "We hung the dummy on a rope from the front of the stage and it just swung around. It would swing around for no reason. At one point, it started to fall, to burn through like someone was burning the rope, but there was nothing—no heat on the rope whatsoever. Nothing and no one was up there in a position to burn it like that."

It has never become clear what caused that anomaly. Perhaps Chester or Isabel, the other well-known ghost who haunts the theater, did not approve of the decorations.

Isabel is the spirit of a teenaged girl. The people who work at the Ventura are extremely fond of her. Nathan, who thinks of himself as something of a ghost hunter even when he's not at work in the haunted theater, explained that the young woman was "killed when she was on stage being crowned as Prom Queen. A piece of lighting equipment dropped [from overhead] and decapitated her."

Judging by her habits as a ghost, Isabel must have died so suddenly that she hasn't yet realized that she's no longer alive. Or perhaps her spirit may just be content to eternally relive the happy first hours of what became a tragic night.

"You can see her walking at stage right once in a while," Nathan said. "She walks toward the stage and down the dance floor. She'll come up and stand next to you. She doesn't try to harm you. She's wearing a really elegant dress, either whitish in color or an extremely light pink."

Dustin has seen her too. He added, "It's kind of weird. She's on stage, usually. To me, Isabel seemed more like a shadow than a real girl."

On a website he created, Phil, the bartender at the Ventura, described some of his encounters with the ghost. On the evening of Saturday, April 25, 1998, Phil postponed an attempt to contact Isabel in her spirit world because a high-school prom was about to be held in the theater. Good thing he did, because Isabel's ghost apparently wanted to attend the dance, not the séance. Phil noted that Nathan watched in awe as a mysterious image of a girl matching Isabel's description walked onto the dance floor to join the others at their prom.

When the party was over and the youngsters had left, Ventura employees set to work dismantling the special decorations. Sometime later, when the stagehands had gone home, the theater was empty. Totally empty. Perhaps even Isabel and Chester had returned to their plane of existence.

All was dark once more, save the ghost light.

One of the Ten Most Haunted

When asked to talk about the ghosts at the Bird Cage Theatre, owner Bill Hunley hardly knows where to begin. His dilemma is certainly understandable, considering that the theater in Tombstone, Arizona, is more than a century old and is also one of the most haunted places in North America. Given the background of the Bird Cage (and all of Tombstone, for that matter), it's no wonder so many restless spirits are seen, felt and heard in the place. The theater was built in 1881, just four years after abundant silver deposits were discovered in the area.

The town's unique name can be traced back to words of advice given to a pioneer miner named Ed Scheffelin. When he indicated that he'd come to the area to find his fortune, he was told that the only thing he was going to find was his own tombstone. Scheffelin immortalized that prediction by naming his claim "Tombstone Mine," and the town, legend has it, simply grew from there.

As a thriving metropolis, Tombstone's heyday was spirited but brief. The town boomed in the 1880s, offering residents and passersby alike all the comforts of home— even a few comforts that might not have been available in some more staid hometowns. The Bird Cage Theatre played an important role, for it was much more than just a theater.

"It was a brothel," Mr. Hunley explained, "an opera-house saloon. The entertainment was very risqué. It was a house for [male patrons] only. Some of the greatest

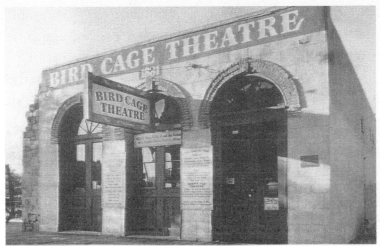

The Bird Cage Theatre in Tombstone is one of the most haunted places in North America.

performers of the 19th century performed there. It was the number one playhouse between St. Louis and San Francisco."

Some of the greatest outlaws of the day—the Earp brothers, Bat Masterson, Jesse James, Wild Bill Hickok and Doc Holliday, to name a few—also performed at the Bird Cage, although probably not on the stage. The gunmen were more likely at the bar or the gambling tables, or with a practitioner of the world's oldest profession in one of the 14 small rooms suspended from the ceiling (which came to be known as Bird Cages). Given the deadly marksmanship of these men, it's no wonder the Bird Cage Theatre is full of ghosts.

Bill Hunley explained, "We have anywhere from 100 to 150 [ghost] sightings a year." In addition, other encounters with spirits "happen so often" to people familiar with the unique building. "I'm around it all the time, so I don't pay that much attention."

Phantom sounds are heard throughout the building.

Ghostly echoes of enthusiastically played card games still reverberate. Musical performances given long ago continue to be heard occasionally.

Mr. Hunley pointed out that at "different times of the year, the ghosts are more active than others. It's in the fall when the weather changes from being very, very warm. It just gets chilly almost overnight…that's when you have the ghost activity—usually October, November or December."

One of the most commonly reported sightings takes place on the theater's stage. An image presumed to be a stagehand "walks from stage right to stage left," Hunley explained. "He's wearing pinstriped pants and carrying a clipboard. He's intently looking at the clipboard. You see him for about a second, maybe a second and a half, then he's gone."

Bill Hunley has witnessed the stagehand's walk to and from eternity several times. But, unlike others, he has never seen the ghost of his own grandfather, who died in 1964 "at nearly a hundred years of age" with a lifetime of involvement with the theater behind him.

Bill continued, "He's been sighted by employees three times, always by new employees. One day, one of our employees was waiting across the street in the post office for the manager to come and open the theater. She got her mail from the post office and was standing there at a table looking down the street at the Bird Cage while she was going through her mail. She saw a white-haired man with a white shirt come out of the Bird Cage. He looked up the street and down the street and then he turned around and went back inside. The employee thought, *Oh my gosh, I'm late. They're open over there.* So she ran across the street, but when she got there the door was locked. The padlock was still on the door."

Bill chuckled as he came to the punch line of this ghost story. "About three or four days later, that same employee came down to the big house where my family's been living since 1884. There's a big picture of my grandfather on the wall and she's said, 'That's the man who walked out of the Bird Cage!' She didn't stay in our employ very long after that—maybe about another month."

During Christmas 2000, there was a sighting of Bill's grandfather and also his grandmother.

"My general manager was closing the theater for the night. She was upstairs and she looked into the auditorium, to the gambling casino, and she saw this older gentleman all dressed up. She didn't remember him coming through and so she asked, 'Can I help you?' He said, 'I'm looking for my wife.' She laughed and said, 'Well, I tell you what. It would be kind of hard to lose her in this building. She's probably in the basement because you exit through the basement. I'm going to the basement anyway.' She walked down the backstage stairs with him. He's behind her. And, there's this older lady standing on the floor at the lower level. She says, 'Ma'am, is this your husband?' And now there's about six or seven people standing there at the landing. She turned around and he had disappeared."

If the folks who witnessed the general manager's conversation with an apparently invisible entity had experienced ghostly encounters of their own in the Bird Cage, at least they would have been understanding.

Other ghostly occurrences at the only theater in Tombstone include the heavy lingering odors of whiskey and cigar smoke, as well as poker chips and cigarette lighters, that appear and then disappear without any rational explanation. The otherworldly pranks have been known to interfere with Bill Hunley's plans, but by now he knows better than to become upset by them. After all, not only does he own an extremely haunted theater but his home is also haunted.

"I grew up in that house and the ghosts have been there since I was a kid."

No wonder the man only has difficulty deciding *which* of his ghost stories to share on any given day.

SCENE IV

George and the Manitoba Theatre Centre

"MTC"—Winnipeg's Manitoba Theatre Centre—is a dynamic and unique institution that dates back some 40 years. Over the years, it has developed a large and loyal following—so loyal, in fact, that when the company moved from its original home in the old Dominion Theatre, everyone, including staff, patrons and resident ghost, went along to the new venue.

"I've never seen him," Teena Laird, a longtime MTC employee, remarked recently. "I feel his presence. Others have seen him, though."

Perhaps because he has been sighted, the theater staff are convinced that the ghost is George, the adolescent son of a former caretaker at the Dominion. George and his father lived in rooms above the old theater. The boy used a wheelchair to get around and, when a fire broke out in the theater building, the poor lad was trapped. His earthly life ended in the blaze but, to this day, George's spirit haunts the Manitoba Theatre Centre.

For the first couple of years after the company moved to its current location, theater employees presumed they had left George behind. Then, one day, it became obvious that the spirit was back among them.

"It was like he was searching for us. It took a while for him to come here. It didn't happen in the first year."

Staff members were glad to have the youngster's spirit back in their midst. Teena explained, "He's friendly, he won't harm you, but he's mischievous just like a boy his age might be. For instance, things will disappear for a time and then, after you've been searching for whatever it is that's missing and you get exasperated, there it will be right by your hand. Filing can be difficult with George around. He'll take the very file you need and it will disappear. You just can't find it for a while. Then it just shows up."

George once joined a group of theater employees during an impromptu social break.

"[We] were socializing, just chatting, and all of a sudden a calculator started working...as though there'd been a power surge, except that it kept on working. It was like he was trying to join our conversation," Ms. Laird recalled.

George's choice to use an electrically connected source is not surprising. Those in the spirit world are clearly drawn to things electrical and electronic. A widely held theory contends that a ghost is the essence or energy of a person left behind after death. If this is correct, then ghosts' attraction to external sources of energy is most understandable.

George did not make an appearance to the group that day, but theater designer Peter Wingate from New York sees the spirit occasionally when he's been working late at night, presumably alone in the theater. Wingate apparently accepts George's presence as one of the benefits of his association with the Winnipeg theater.

Even Wingate's commendably accepting attitude might have been jostled a little had he witnessed George's stunt with the theater seats. Teena remembered the day when MTC was still located in the Dominion Theatre and "All the seats were down…and [then] it was like someone was running down the rows, flipping the seats up."

Teena's curiosity was piqued. She actually crawled under the seats to search for a clue as to what might have caused such an anomaly. Of course, there was nothing— nothing visible, that is.

By now, George is as much a part of MTC as are stellar performances. Teena explained that, while outsiders might find the behavior odd, she and other staff members make a point of talking to George throughout the day. New employees at the Manitoba Theatre Centre can be skeptical and find the staff's habit of speaking to a phantom amusing. Such an attitude of disbelief doesn't usually last too long. Once they witness a ghostly prank or two, their skepticism quickly dissolves.

To justify her determined stance that there is a ghost in the theater, Laird described a time when she needed to find two particular receipts. It was not going to be easy, but it was very important that the documents be found. Teena knew whom she had to call on for help and, moments after making her request, the receipts fluttered into an otherwise empty wastepaper basket.

George is not this helpful to everyone, however. He once took a dislike to a certain actor and made the man's life miserable. Another time, George interfered with a stage setting by throwing books that were being used as props off the shelves where they'd been placed.

Despite these annoyances, George is an integral and respected part of the Manitoba Theatre Centre. Teena Laird, who is constantly aware of the ghost's presence, concluded by stating emphatically, "We believe in this very strongly."

Perhaps George should take a ghostly bow for his involvement in the theater.

SCENE V

The Tommy Gilbert Story

A collection of photographs hangs in the lobby of the Gulfport Little Theatre. Most of the photos depict the earliest productions of the theater when staging each show was a feat to be celebrated. Amidst the more standard framed photographs is one of an empty and apparently ordinary soda pop bottle placed on a concrete slab that lies abandoned in an otherwise barren field.

Of course, every picture has a story. Theater associate George Leggett begins by explaining that, in the mid-1940s, a "group of aspiring actors got together and produced a few plays. Twenty years later, after saving what money they could, they were able to build their first theater." They leased the land on which their new building stood from "the city, for the princely sum of a dollar each year."

Many residents of Gulfport, Mississippi, including radio announcer Tommy Gilbert, were active in the Little

Theatre productions. On his popular radio program, Tommy billed himself as "the morning mayor." His many listeners looked forward to starting their day by hearing the unique disc jockey's effervescent greeting of "good morning, good morning, good morning. The sun is shining and it's a beautiful day! When you're in town today, be sure and stop by…" followed by his recommendations of what stops might be particularly interesting on any given day.

During his leisure time, Tommy Gilbert devoted himself just as enthusiastically to the Gulfport Little Theatre. In his position as radio announcer, it was easy for him to publicize upcoming plays, but he also helped to build sets and even took an occasional turn as a performer.

With the help of Tommy Gilbert and many others, all was going well for the newly built theater until August 17, 1969—the day that Camille, a Category 5 hurricane, crossed the coast of the state of Mississippi. That was the day the Little Theatre members found out that the lease rate was not such a bargain after all: the land was too close to the beach. There was no protection from severe onshore weather. Hurricane Camille, with winds exceeding 200 miles (320 kilometers) an hour, leveled the theater building in mere seconds. All that remained of the hard work that had gone into building the place was the concrete slab on which it had stood.

There was no question that the Little Theatre would be re-established—"safely away from the tidal surge," as George Leggett specified—but rebuilding took a tremendous amount of effort from a great number of devoted people. Tommy Gilbert was among those who worked tirelessly to replace what had been lost.

Sadly, less than a decade later, Tommy died. The staff at the radio station where he'd worked so happily for so many years wanted to create a lasting memorial to the "morning mayor." It wasn't much of a stretch to see that it would be fitting to connect the memorial for Tommy Gilbert with the Little Theatre he loved. So the radio station staff donated "a statuette of two dolphins, requesting it be used every year to honor the person who had done the most for the theater [and] naming it the Tommy Gilbert Award." Thus the man was forever linked to the theater.

Tommy Gilbert's soul, however, did not need anything so physical as a statuette to tie him to the theater for eternity. Leggett explained, "When a crew is working late, there will be a sound in the dark auditorium and someone is certain to remark, 'Don't worry about it, it's only Tommy.' "

But what about the strange framed photograph of the pop bottle? The bottle is not of a kind that is currently available but is from a brand of soda that used to be stocked in the drink machine in the old theater—the building that Tommy Gilbert loved and that Hurricane Camille destroyed.

The bottle was found at center stage of the new theater on an October evening after the awards ceremony in which the Tommy Gilbert trophy was first presented. "No one knew where it came from," George Leggett recalled before explaining that even more mysterious than the curious object itself was the fact that "the bottle was not empty. Tucked inside was a note with a hastily scrawled message." The note read simply, "Thanks for remembering," and was signed, "Tommy."

Haunting Horace

The year, 1879. The place, Leadville, Colorado, roughly 110 miles (180 kilometers) southwest of the growing metropolis of Denver. Leadville's raison d'être was mining. Abundant veins of silver formed crisscross patterns under the ground surrounding the Wild West town, and ambitious miners populated it in droves.

Horace A.W. Tabor was one of Leadville's leading citizens, having established a profitable business mining the miners. He was a retailer in a boom town where every resident was a recent arrival who needed to purchase the goods necessary to get established as quickly as possible. Without either the time or the facilities available for comparison shopping, miners paid exhorbitant retail prices. With the profits from his store, and the wise investments made with those profits, Tabor soon became a very wealthy man.

Unlike the majority of Leadville residents, material wealth was not enough for Horace. He missed the entertainment and refinement he had enjoyed before making his way west. Returning east to an established cultural hot spot was not an option, so the rich man was left with no choice but to import culture to his new hometown. And so it was, on a chilly November night in 1879, that a crowd gathered for the opening of the Tabor Opera House.

Today, well over a century later, the theater still stands. Its owner, Evelyn Furman, also acts as historian and tour guide.

"One day, included in a group touring the theater was a middle-aged couple that I shall never forget. They were conservative in dress and had a quiet and reserved manner," Miss Furman recalled. "As usual, I led the group of tourists up and down the aisles, through the dressing rooms, on to the stage, under the stage and up into the balcony. I talked to the group when we stopped at each station. All were interested in the history of Leadville, the Opera House and especially Tabor himself."

Evelyn Furman continued, "The couple I mentioned previously listened intently. As we neared the end of the tour, we stood under the balcony near the theater entrance. Everyone crowded close to me, not wanting to miss a word of the tour.

"After the tour, the couple came to me and asked if I had ever seen any strange things or ghosts in the Tabor Opera House. I answered, 'No.' The man, in a very serious voice said, 'I saw a rather heavy-set middle-aged man standing near you while you were talking…right there under the balcony near a pillar. He was dark complected, had a mustache and wore a good watch and chain.'

"I was astonished and surprised to think they saw this person. I saw no one there beside me. The description fit H.A.W. Tabor perfectly."

Unfortunately, with all the duties that Evelyn Furman has in connection with the theater, she was as busy that day as she usually is. She had no time either to let the revelation that she'd just been privy to settle in, or to speak further with the obviously sensitive couple. "I had to take the next tour. They were waiting."

Apparently Evelyn Furman isn't as alone carrying out her responsibilities in the theater as she thought she was.

An Eternal Usher

Richard Douglas Miller's short life was a sad one. So sad, in fact, that on February 5, 1967, at the age of 18, Dick Miller, as he was known to friends and family, decided to end it all.

At first glance, Dick was an unlikely candidate for suicide. He was a college student, the son of a well-to-do family. His father was a doctor practicing in a suburb of St. Paul, Minnesota. Out of concern for the quality of their son's education, Dr. and Mrs. Miller insisted that the young man quit his part-time job to concentrate his time and efforts on school work. Their reasoning seemed sound, especially as they were able and willing to support their son financially.

Unfortunately, in their attempt to relieve what they perceived as unnecessary pressure in Dick's life, his parents relieved him of the activity that made him feel most worthy as a human being. The Millers had no idea how much pleasure their son experienced in donning his usher's uniform and assisting patrons of the Guthrie Theatre to their seats. When he realized that his parents' demands were unshakable, Dick accepted their determination. But he could not accept the outcome of their decision, because he knew it would mean the end of the most satisfying element of his life.

Apparently unable to think of a less permanent solution to the dilemma, Dick plotted his own death. He asked his mother to lend him her car and some money.

Mrs. Miller didn't know it at the time, but the amount of Dick's loan request was just enough to cover the cost of his suicide. The car would provide the venue for his self-inflicted destruction.

In his Guthrie Theatre uniform, Dick drove through snow-clogged streets to a local department store on Lake Street. There he purchased an inexpensive used rifle and a box of shells. He returned to the car, loaded the rifle, put it against his head and pulled the trigger. Richard Douglas Miller's problems, on this plane of existence, were over. His body lay in the car for roughly 36 hours before an unfortunate department store employee stumbled upon the results of Miller's depression.

Dick died instantly, his skull fragmented by the point-blank shot. There was never any question of another cause of death except suicide. He had even left a carefully penned note of explanation. It informed the living that "ushering was the best thing I've ever done." He asked that he be buried in his uniform and that his theater colleagues do him the final honor of acting as pallbearers. His requests were granted. Given this sudden and tragic insight into their son's anguish, Dr. and Mrs. Miller asked that mourners remember young Dick's short and unhappy life with a donation to the local mental health association.

Though he acquiesced to parental authority so unquestioningly in life, Dick Miller demonstrated a decidedly willful nature after death. Just weeks after his death, a member of an audience at the Guthrie Theatre complained that she had been distracted from the show she'd been enjoying. She said an usher kept pacing the aisle during a performance. The theater manager was concerned to receive such a complaint, especially as he knew that there were no ushers in the auditorium during the performance. He asked the woman to describe the person she'd seen. The offended patron described Dick Miller in painstaking detail, right down to the large mole on his cheek.

That strange incident stood in isolation until Thanksgiving 1968 when three teenaged employees at the theater decided to bring a Ouija board into the Guthrie. Dan, Bruce and Scott worked their shifts as always, but at the end of the evening, rather than leaving for home, the boys found hiding places in the mammoth old building. They waited until they were sure everyone else had left before emerging from their hiding spots, Ouija board in hand.

Apart from adolescent curiosity, what motivated the lads to such a foolish act is not known. Whatever their reasons might have been, the group's patience wasn't tested by the paranormal experiment. Moments after the three had placed their fingertips on the board's planchette, it began to move about. Initially, they could discern nothing comprehensible but, once the pointer calmed down, it was clear they had been successful in contacting a spirit.

Although the board misspelled Dick's last name, it let the boys know that they were not alone. Young Bruce's reaction to the message has been lost to time and Scott was, at first, blissfully ignorant of its implications. He hadn't known Dick. Dan, however, was deeply affected. The color drained from his face as he followed the directions spelled out by the Ouija. Dan and the others looked up and, for the first time in their young lives, saw a ghost.

The slightly shimmering image of Richard Douglas Miller, dressed in his Guthrie Theatre usher's uniform, stood suspended beside the theater's lighting booth.

Predictably, the teens were terrified by the success of their amateur séance but, by the time Scott returned to work the next evening, he'd become more comfortable with the experience. He allowed his mind to remain open to the possibility of seeing the ghost again. His positive thinking apparently worked because he and the late Dick Miller became, in a strange way, work mates.

Miller always appeared in the distance, in a slightly ethereal form and dressed in the uniform that meant so much to him in life. Scott became so accustomed to seeing the image that, on the days he caught a glimpse of the usher-from-beyond, he would call out a friendly greeting to the apparition. Although the ghost never responded to the salutation, it seemed to be very much aware of the living and watched Scott perform his duties with apparent interest.

Eventually Scott left the employ of the Guthrie Theatre. Dick Miller, of course, did not. Since then, others have also seen the spirit but not everyone has been quite as calm about the haunting as Scott was. A lighting technician, getting off an elevator in the building, ran back to the security of the lift when he realized that the man he'd just seen wearing an usher's uniform had been transparent.

The most bizarre sighting of the ghost of Dick Miller took place outside the theater. An actress performing at the Guthrie reported that as she drove in front of the old place, she suddenly had a passenger in her car—Dick Miller. The eternally young man must have liked this particular woman because he came to watch her rehearse one day. When she saw the figure, the actress incorrectly presumed that her solitary audience member was a living employee. She began to address her lines directly to him. Apparently her performance didn't hold his attention because as she watched, the human-like form disappeared as quickly as it had appeared.

When the theater was renovated in the early 1990s, the Guthrie's administration called in a man known for his ability to direct spirits from this world to their own. The exorcism must have been a success because, since the Guthrie Theatre reopened, there have been no further sightings of Dick Miller. For this reason it seems unlikely that his spirit will return—even if, as is a possibility at this writing, the owners of the facility replace it with a new auditorium.

Jane's Home

Jane is not just one of those nameless, vague presences who's *thought* to haunt a theater. No way. People know Jane. They know her name and are also able to recognize her personality characteristics. Jane is so well accepted on the University of North Carolina's Greensboro campus that those associated with Aycock Auditorium even acknowledge her ghostly, and annoying, faults. None of this acceptance is really too much of a surprise considering that Jane has enjoyed a long and active tenure on campus, thereby giving people associated with the theater lots of opportunity to get to know her.

Men generally have one of two rather interesting reactions to Jane. Some men go out of their way to catch a glimpse of her. Others put an equal amount of effort into avoiding any chance of seeing Jane. Women, however, don't face the same choices. You see, no female has ever seen Jane's ghost.

It is generally accepted that Jane is the spirit of a woman who, in the early 1900s, lived in a house located on the corner of Spring Garden and Tate Streets—exactly where the theater now stands. The woman, whose name may or may not have been "Jane," was tragically lonely and eventually took her own life.

Theater professor Tom Behm met Jane in 1988 while he was directing the musical *Bye Bye Birdie*. Because Behm had been associated with the university for many years by that time, it is likely that he was well aware of the theater's ghost stories. Despite such forewarning, Behm was badly shaken when the phantom seemed to approach him as he came back into the empty theater to retrieve his briefcase.

It was nearly midnight and most of the lights were turned off when Behm entered the haunted theater. As he approached the stage, "lights started to come up and flash on and off," he told Cathy Gant-Hill, a reporter for the Greensboro *News & Record*. Once Jane had the man's attention, she appeared in front of him as a white, vaporous image. The smoke-like cloud crossed the stage, floated down the steps and continued on toward the professor. The sight was enough to send Behm hurrying out into the night, promising himself that he would never be in the theater alone again.

Seven years after Behm's frightening experience, Lyman Collins, manager of the Aycock Auditorium, purposely set himself up for an encounter with the specter. Collins' timing was deliberate—and rewarding. He chose to go ghost hunting at dusk on Halloween in 1995. The theater was dark except for the ghost light on the stage. That fixture—designed to offer a bit of security to anyone entering an empty theater—was to blame for Collins' first scare. When he first glanced at the stage, the orange electrical cord supplying power to the single bulb set atop a tripod looked like a "trail of blood." Seconds later, the man regained his composure and realized that his eyes were simply playing tricks on him.

After searching the house for Jane, Lyman was about to give up his ghost hunt and leave. That was when he heard it—a single note being played on a piano. As he knew that he was alone in a locked building, the man rushed to investigate the sound he'd heard. He soon spotted the piano—but the instrument was not in its usual place. Workers had moved it out of their way and into an aisle. Once Lyman calmed down from his musical ghostly encounter, he decided that Jane was not trying to frighten him but was just trying to draw attention to herself and to the fact that the piano was not where it should be.

Theater student Jeff Neubauer also had an encounter with Jane in the fall of 1995. He and a friend were securing the building for the night when the ghost decided to casually stroll past them. Jeff described the entity as being "a very fair" woman "with light-colored hair."

About that time, another student, Michael Marlowe, was alone in the basement of the theater. He was working with some props when he felt a hand being placed firmly on his shoulder. He swung around to see who had joined him—but no one was there.

In 1997, Michael was treated to an actual sighting of Jane. Again, he was alone in the basement. This time, he didn't feel any pressure on his shoulder. He merely stood and watched, in awe, as the same white cloud that the others had described made its way into the sunken orchestra pit.

Those familiar with Jane feel that, in addition to preferring men rather than any women who've ever worked at the theater, Jane also prefers operas over other types of theatrical productions. She also likes to get involved in staging productions. In fact, Jane has played with the electrical lights in the theater so often over the years that one of the switches on the theater's lighting board is known as "Jane's dimmer."

And so, although Jane originally had nothing to do with the university or with the theater itself, over the years she's clearly made that "house" her home.

Ford's Theatre

Great controversy surrounds the proposition that Ford's Theatre in Washington, D.C., is haunted. As the site of Abraham Lincoln's assassination, the building certainly has every right to have at least one ghost. There are many people, however, who feel strongly that the place is not haunted. They say that it couldn't possibly be; after all, according to them, it isn't even the same building. With equal conviction, others maintain they know that it's haunted because they've seen the ghosts.

United States National Parks historian and disbeliever Michael Maione explained that the theater originally opened on August 27, 1863, after five months of construction work. Although the total cost was an astronomical $75,000, the investors expected to recoup their expenses over time. They had no way of knowing that, less than a year and a half later, their contribution to the performing arts community would become the venue for a tragedy that would alter the course of United States history.

On the evening of April 14, 1865, during a performance of the play *Our American Cousin*, John Wilkes Booth, an out-of-work actor, approached Box 7 at Ford's Theatre, drew his Derringer pistol and fired repeatedly at the president's head. As the sounds of the shots echoed through the auditorium, panic spread through the audience. Booth vaulted from the raised seating area to the stage below, breaking a bone in his leg as he landed. Limping badly, he scattered the confused and horrified actors as he made his escape across the stage and out of the theater, leaving the 16th president of the United States of America dying.

Historian Maione explained, "The play didn't finish that evening," or ever again for that matter. The play, like the theater itself, had become irrevocably tainted. Just days later, however, investigators wanting to recreate the crime scene as closely as possible had the actors replay their roles, but only up to the lines that were being spoken when the fatal shots were fired. At that point, the authorities halted the performance and followed the escapee's path to temporary freedom. Actors never set foot on that stage again.

"Within a few weeks, the YMCA announced it intended to reopen the theater as the Abraham Lincoln Theater," Maione continued. The public apparently was not ready for such a resurrection. No one would commit the necessary financial support and the project ended before it had begun.

In 1866 the government bought the building from the Ford brothers for $100,000 and, according to Maione, "walked in and gutted it." In 1867 the building reopened as a three-story government office building where clerks earned their living by processing official documents. For more than 25 years, the address that had been the site of that terrible tragedy steadily earned its way out of infamy—until June 9, 1893.

"Between 9:30 and 10:00 [AM on that day] the building collapse[d] like an accordion," Michael Maione said. Twenty-two men died and sixty were injured. (At that point in history, a woman was not permitted to hold a job

as responsible as a clerical position with the government.)
Rumors immediately flourished. The building was jinxed,
many opined. People said the horrible accident had been
caused by Lincoln's spirit coming back to destroy the
place where he had been murdered. Still others agreed
there was a jinx on the place and that this second tragedy
was of paranormal origins, but they held that it was
caused by the ghost of John Wilkes Booth.

Despite such fears, simple economics dictated that the
site would continue to be used. Even in the 1800s, land in
the United States' capital was too valuable to sit empty
and, in 1894, a three-story warehouse was erected. "No
offices, no theater," historian Maione stated flatly.

By the early 1930s, a movement began among the general population to promote the idea that Lincoln's memory should somehow be preserved at this historic location. Eventually the first floor of the warehouse was
transformed into a museum dedicated to the memory of
President Lincoln. The commemorative display opened
on February 12, 1932, 133 years to the day after the
esteemed leader's birth. According to Maione, organizers
incorporated into the display "really weird, big fat yellow,
footprints showing the route Booth took" when he fled
the theater. The second and third floors of the building
continued to be used as a storage facility.

Then, in 1945, United States Senator Milton R. Young
visited the museum and asked, as Maione paraphrased,
"Guys, where's the theater?" The man's query lead to a
campaign to raise the funds necessary to recreate Ford's
Theatre as it existed on that fateful spring evening in 1865.
On June 21, 1968, the building reopened as a replica of the

original theater. Box 7, where Lincoln sat the night he was killed, is permanently roped off and stands, frozen in time, as a tribute to the president's memory.

Builders referred to archival photographs to determine architectural accuracy. If some of those photos were the ones taken by Civil War photographer Matthew Brady shortly after Lincoln's assassination, the workers may have noted an indistinct image in the otherwise vacant Box 7. Those who saw that photograph swore that Brady had captured the phantom reflection of John Wilkes Booth, for the picture showed a shadowy form crouched beside the chair on which Lincoln had been sitting when he was killed. History has not recorded whether photographer Brady saw the image either before or after he took the picture but, even at that time, others did report seeing images in the theater that they swore were not of this world.

Similar reports continue today. Many people become unnerved when they walk into one of the highly localized, and seemingly unexplainable, pockets of cold air scattered throughout the theater. Such a phenomenon is generally associated with the presence of a ghost. Others have heard phantom footsteps echoing from areas of the theater known to be empty. These sounds are said to be distinctively heavy steps, the kind a person would make wearing boots such as the ones Booth wore the night he murdered the president. The footfalls are typically heard during certain acts of specific plays and not at other times. There has even been a sighting of a phantom boot levitating over the sealed-off Presidential Box 7.

The phantom footsteps are apparently not the eeriest

sounds, though. Inexplicable laughter that occasionally echoes throughout Ford's Theatre is reported to be the most unnerving. Those ghostly giggles so frightened a stagehand while he was changing his clothes that he fled from the theater—clad only in his underwear.

The stage area of Ford's Theatre is said to be extremely haunted. The curtain rises and falls as if it had a will of its own and, on the stage itself, there is apparently a distinct pattern of paranormal energy. Actors have named this path the "occult line" and go to great lengths to avoid walking into it. Stepping into this area can bring on feelings of illness, extreme nervousness, as well as an actor's worst nightmare—amnesia. These unpleasant and area-specific sensations cannot be written off as excuses offered by inexperienced actors because reports have come from some legends of live theater including Hal Holbrook. It's probably no coincidence that this corridor of negative paranormal energy follows John Wilkes Booth's escape route from the theater. (Although Booth did make his way from the scene of his crime that night, he did not evade justice for long: less than two weeks later the assassin was also dead.)

Booth may not be alone in the afterworld of Ford's Theatre. Lights have been seen flickering on and off in Box 7, although the reconstructed presidential seating area is cordoned off and has never been used. A lecturer delivering a presentation about Abraham Lincoln maintained that, while giving his address in Ford's Theatre, he looked up at Box 7 and saw a ghostly image of the long-deceased political leader sitting in his accustomed chair, listening to the speech.

Historian Michael Maione would disagree, but that has to be expected from an admitted skeptic. John Alexander's report in his book, *Ghosts: Washington's Most Famous Ghost Stories*, is a little more surprising. Alexander maintains that, while the ghost of Abraham Lincoln does exist, it only haunts the White House.

Perhaps we mortals may never know for certain how many, if any, presences reside in the landmark theater. That being the case, then the debate will continue, possibly into eternity.

There are two lesser-known but equally eerie paranormal events that are loosely associated with the Lincoln assassination. General Ulysses S. Grant and his wife Julia had been visiting the Lincolns on that fateful day in April 1865. They were to accompany the president and Mrs. Lincoln to the play. As Friday morning progressed toward noon, Mrs. Grant developed an increasingly strong urge to leave Washington and begin their journey home.

During the noon hour, a rather strange and unexpected messenger came to the Grants' hotel room with a reminder that they were to join the Lincolns that evening. Rather than prompting Julia Grant to ignore her sense of foreboding and commit to the invitation, the man's visit only served to increase her resolve to leave the city as soon as possible. The general was in a very difficult position: even though he was himself an esteemed leader in the country, it was not easy, wise or polite to turn down an invitation from the president. In the end, Grant relented and accepted that his wife's feelings could not be ignored. By the time the Lincolns were settling into their date with destiny, the Grants were out of the capital.

It wasn't until the next day that General Grant learned that the president had been assassinated and that John Wilkes Booth had intended to kill him too. Were it not for his wife's insistence that they heed the foreboding she felt, General Ulysses S. Grant would probably also have been killed that night.

In a further irony, if Abraham Lincoln had attended the play of *his* preference on that spring evening, the assassination might not have occurred, the president might have lived out his term and the original Ford's Theatre might still stand—unhaunted—exactly as it did before April 14, 1865.

It was Mary Todd Lincoln, the president's wife, who wanted to see the Ford's Theatre production of *Our American Cousin*. Lincoln had apparently expressed a preference for the show being presented at the nearby National Theatre—another auditorium that eventually earned a reputation as being haunted.

During that era, stage actors were not held in such high regard as actors are today. They were poorly paid and most lived in poverty. Performing at the National Theatre offered something of an unintended benefit for impoverished actors. A sewer line ran directly under the stage, and it was said that thespians often slipped down there, sometimes between performances, to wash their clothes.

It is also said that one of these clandestine and probably most unpleasant laundry bees took place in 1885 during a run of the play *Hamlet*. An argument developed, a physical fight ensued and an actor named John McCullough was killed. His murderer buried the body immediately and no doubt hoped that no questions would be asked about what happened to McCullough or, perhaps more importantly, to the costume he had been wearing.

Legend has it that, throughout the following years, an apparition dressed as a character from *Hamlet* has been seen around the theater. The image never speaks. He just looks around the set before indicating his approval with a nod or his disapproval with a scowl. He then vanishes as mysteriously as he appeared.

In keeping with theater tradition, those associated with the National are very protective of this ghost. In the early 1930s, a suggestion that the body be exhumed and given a "proper" burial was met with an overwhelmingly negative response. It was pointed out that an actor could not ask for a more suitable final resting spot than one within a theater and so, as far as my research indicates, John McCullough's body, and his ghost, continue to be sheltered in Washington's National Theatre.

Another strange twist of ghostly fate has John Wilkes Booth's brother Edwin haunting the Springer Opera House in Columbus, Georgia. On February 15, 1876, Edwin Booth, also an actor, played the lead role in *Hamlet*. His performance astounded the members of the audience who were fortunate enough to attend the one-time production, and his spirit is still in residence playing ghostly tricks on current Opera House employees. Booth is generally credited, or blamed, depending on the worker's attitude, for rearranging keys and costumes, for opening and closing doors and for causing eerie music to be heard throughout the building when the place was known to be empty.

The ghost stories connected with Lincoln's assassination seem to be as puzzling as they are varied!

Possessed Piano?

Robert Loucks, the former artistic director at a haunted theater called Unchagah Hall in Dawson Creek, British Columbia, was living only a few blocks from me when he wrote to let me know of his conversion from skeptic to believer as a result of his paranormal experiences at that theater.

In a subsequent interview, Robert began by explaining that right from the time he first arrived at the job, he'd heard that the performance hall was haunted. "Of course I didn't believe in ghosts, so I didn't pay much attention to the ghost story." He went on to describe the hall as being a "large (over 600 seats), legitimate theatre that was rumored to have been built on an old Indian burial site."

The man never attempted to confirm or refute the legend, but he did know that, by September 1990, when he came away from his employment in northern British Columbia, his belief system had been substantially altered by his encounters with the spirit residing in the theater. And it's not much wonder because, as Robert stated, "it's quite a story," before adding, "I'll start from the beginning."

The word *unchagah* means "peace" in the Beaver language, the man explained. The theater's name, therefore, was somewhat ironic when the ghost was active, because at those times the atmosphere in the building would become seriously disrupted.

"The ghost kicked up quite a fuss in January 1980, when I came to the theater. The first while, I spent a lot of time in my office at nights when no one else was there. I would hear doors banging and I would go and I would look, but there was nobody else in the building."

Still more concerned with learning the duties involved in his new position, Robert didn't attempt to track down the strange sounds. Not long after his tenure began, however, Robert's daughter had an unexplained and extremely unnerving experience in the basement of the theater.

"My daughter, Troy, who was about 17 years old at the time, was helping me one night. She went downstairs [to the basement], which was this huge place. We called it 'The Dungeon' because it was almost completely unexcavated except for one small room at the end. That was the room we built sets in."

The Dungeon may have been unexcavated, but it was not empty. "The whole thing was filled with old theater sets. It was eerie. You walked over mounds of earth. It was like going up and down mountains and the area it covered was just enormous. I don't think I ever did know every corner of it. My daughter was down there when, suddenly, all the lights went off. I don't know how she ever made her way out. She didn't even have a flashlight. I was in the building, but I didn't know [she was in difficulty]. Finally she found her way out and, when she did, she was quite quiet. To this day, we don't know why those lights would've gone out, but lights do figure in this story as it goes on."

At the time, neither Robert nor his daughter had any way of knowing that they were embarking on what was to be a most interesting journey. The ghost was just *starting* to show both its presence and its strength.

As part of his responsibilities with the theater, Robert taught drama classes to high-school students. After each of these sessions, Loucks would "turn the lights off and give the kids a relaxation exercise." During one of these quiet post-instruction periods, Robert recalled that "someone said, 'Oh, it's eerie in here. You know there's a ghost in here.' I said, 'Just forget it. There's no ghost. Relax.' "

After a moment's pause, the former skeptic continued, "I hardly got the words out of my mouth and a red light came on over the stage. Of course, the kids were quite nonplussed by it, but I just [dismissed] it…by explaining that lights do ghost [leave an aura of illumination after they've been turned off]."

Another of Robert Louck's challenges with the new position revolved around a piano. "There was a Steinway piano and it was always, oh, so much trouble. It had been one of those eternal problems when I took over. It had been badly handled. I had it all redone. It cost thousands of dollars, but I had it all fixed up."

In retrospect, fixing the piano was a most worthwhile investment because, from that moment on, and for the next decade, Robert was able to enjoy his job in the northern community without any interference from otherworldly sources.

"Ten years later, in about May 1990, I put in my resignation. I was going to move to Edmonton," Robert explained. Before he left, the man organized a drama festival for young people. It was to take place at Unchagah Hall. As part of the arrangements for this event, the man invited an adjudicator from Vancouver, B.C.

"The first day the participants were there, the adjudicator and I were standing on the stage. He'd been there only a few hours. He said to me, 'Robert, do you know that you have a ghost in here?' I said, 'Yes, there was one years ago but it hasn't been around for a long time.'

"When we finished our tour, we came back. It was about 2:00 or 3:00 in the morning. I stayed with the truck and the kids were starting to unload and take stuff into the theater. One of the girls came to me and said, 'Mr. Loucks, the lights are going on and off,' and I said, 'That's impossible' and she said, 'Well they are.' "

Perhaps realizing that the spirit was back, Robert was not completely surprised by the situation he was literally about to walk into. "I finished what I was doing and I went in. The kids had other lights on the stage, what you call the 'work lights,' but the theater lights, the big lights. They were just…"

The well-spoken man paused before finishing his sentence. He seemed to be trying to capture the best words to describe the scene that had unfolded before his eyes.

"It was like a light show. It was like a rock show. The lights were going on and off all over the place." Robert suspected that they were all in the company of a paranormal force and as the adult in charge he was the one with a decision to make. "I said, very quietly, 'Let's not bother putting the stuff away. We'll just put it on the stage for now.' Then we left and had pizza or something."

The phantom's farewell to Robert Loucks had, unfortunately, just begun.

"For the next couple of weeks, the last two or three weeks I was there, this [bizarre phenomenon with the lights] happened all the time. We even had to sometimes stop shows because we couldn't control the lights. It was unbelievable. We checked the [electrical] boards, we had the electricians in, but nothing seemed to be able to control it."

As Robert continued his reflections, the story became frighteningly dramatic. "One Saturday in this period of time, I was at the hall working. It was dark and I walked on the stage. A light came on. I moved and another light came on. Then I moved once again and another light came on. I moved once again and another light came on. I thought, *Okay, I'm getting out of here*, and I walked over to get off the stage. There was a stairway that went from the stage to where my office was and led to the door to get out [of the building]."

Robert paused, clearly still affected by the experiences from 20 years before. "I *couldn't* get up the stairs. A force kept pushing me down the stairs. I'm not kidding. I had both hands on the stair rail and was pulling myself up, but it was like I was trying to move against a gale wind. I couldn't get up the stairs.

"There was a phone on the stairs and I phoned a young man, one of my actors. He and another fellow came over. They had no trouble [getting into the building], but when they got down the stairs they said, 'Oh boy.' They could really feel the ghost's presence. I guess I could too. They went out into the auditorium and they watched while I walked across the stage. Everywhere I went, the lights followed me. It was unbelievable, but the lights kept coming on me wherever I went. There was nobody in the lighting booth. There was nothing. I mean, the electrical board was turned off, and I had the key."

Robert, as is often the case even with very articulate people, had difficulty describing his encounter with the ghost. "It was a feeling something like electricity going through my body, stronger than goosebumps. It was so palpable, that feeling, the strength of it. The students said, 'The ghost is mad at you, really mad at you.' That's the feeling they had. I think it was mad because I was leaving and I had been the one who had protected that piano, that very old Steinway."

Robert concluded his retelling of that incredible incident by simply stating, "When the force went away, I got off the stage."

But the spirit was not through drawing attention to itself. "Often I would leave the place because I would just think, *No, I'm not staying here tonight.* I'd had enough. The bangings started up again and sometimes the drapes would shake on their own. These were huge, heavy, heavy, heavy drapes and they would actually jump up and down."

These incidents left the normally calm man somewhat shaken. "I phoned a friend of mine who was a white witch. We decided that we would go back [to the theater] on Sunday night—late at midnight or something around there. She got all her paraphernalia together to have a séance."

At this point in the interview, I interjected that I thought such an activity would've taken a great deal of courage. Robert replied, "Well, I guess I am brave, because the woman said, 'Please consider this, Robert. Maybe this isn't a kindly spirit.'"

Despite that warning, the pair continued with their plan. "We did the séance, and not a peep—nothing. The woman couldn't contact anything. It wasn't interested in [coming through] while she was there, even though I spoke and asked, 'What are you trying to tell me? What do you want to say?' "

The results of the séance were undeniably disappointing. Worse, though, was that the "next morning, Monday, late in the morning, the same damned thing started up again. The lights were going on and off. They actually became more frantic, but I didn't know what it [the inexplicable force] wanted. Finally, in June, I think maybe three weeks from the time this whole thing had started again, I left my employment with the theater.

"The theater was closed for the summer but I stayed in town until August. After I left the city, the hall caught on fire. The fire brigade was called and they were able to put the fire out. A few days later, the place caught on fire again. This struck me as being very odd because there was never a fire the whole time I was there. The second blaze did a lot of damage. It burned the whole stage area and the Steinway grand piano went bang down through the stage. This, of course, completely destroyed the instrument."

The incident also took with it any shreds of skepticism that Robert might have clung to. He reported, "I was changed completely." He realized that the ghostly activity had been directly connected to the piano. The phantom was apparently angry until Robert had the Steinway repaired and then quiet until the man had stated his intentions to leave the theater.

Robert Loucks also abandoned his skepticism. Now he is a complete believer, as a result of just one job. One job in a theater with an apparently possessed piano, that is.

PHANTOM
PERFORMANCES

Disturbing Display

Actors, it would seem, don't always have to be in a theater to encounter a paranormal force. Delores Wheeler of Edmond, Oklahoma, wrote to tell me of an inexplicable event that she witnessed.

"I work with a murder-mystery dinner theater group called the Whodunit Dining Room," Delores began, before explaining that the troupe performs at various venues "throughout the state of Oklahoma."

She continued by detailing a particular pre-show occurrence. "At one restaurant in Oklahoma City, we were opening a new show in the spring of 1996. I was sitting in a chair waiting for the show to start. A fellow actor was standing next to me. Suddenly, his [cigarette] lighter flew out of his pants pocket. He thought he must have a hole in his pocket and so he put it in the other side pocket."

Much to the amazement of both Delores and the man whose lighter was "acting" so strangely, the lighter flew out of that pocket too.

"Since I was at eye level [to his pockets], I could clearly see what was happening. The man checked his pockets for holes and found none. [Next] he put the lighter in his shirt pocket. It did the same thing."

Badly unnerved by the odd series of events, but knowing that "the show must go on," Delores and her colleague threw the troublesome lighter in the garbage. Despite this attempt to banish their troubles, she recalled, "We were barely able to say our lines once the show started. Was an invisible prankster with us or does one of us have latent psychokinetic powers? Who knows!"

Further questions could be added to Delores' list. For instance, is the restaurant they were performing in haunted on a full-time basis or was a mischievous spirit simply passing through? It's likely no one will ever have a reasonable explanation for the bizarre, poltergeist-like incident.

SCENE II

Just Call Him "Shorty"

People associated with haunted theaters are often very fond of the ghost who is haunting their "house." The affection felt for "Shorty," the ghost of the Capitol Theatre in Yakima, Washington, goes well beyond the ordinary. Bonnie Hughes, the community relations director, and stage manager Roger Smith both went out of their way to supply me with details of the story about their ghost because they felt it was important, Bonnie specified, that Shorty "get the recognition he deserves."

Roger began to recount his version of the story: "The name of the ghost is 'Shorty.' Simply, 'Shorty.' No first or last name. No one can offer a description of Shorty. Nobody can relate a biography. His activities are manifested mostly when the theater is empty and at rest, between shows. Shorty exists just as surely as the walls of the theater stand to house his unpredictable presence."

Smith detailed one particularly dramatic encounter with their resident presence. "It was 1980 and the Cold War was still raging. A touring dance troupe from what was then Czechoslovakia came to the Capitol Theatre for an evening performance. Security was tight because the dancers were tempted to defect and seek a better life in North America."

He went on, "A performance is heavily dependent on lighting for its aesthetic and dramatic effect. Lighting changes are [made using] a 'cue sheet.' This sheet is often several pages in length, detailing several hundred light changes during a presentation. One of the dances of the Czech group included a choreographed dagger fight between two rival peasants. Before the scene, much to the frustration and panic of the two dancers, one of the steel daggers [was] missing from the prop table on stage right. In a baffling coincidence, page 13 of the lighting cue sheet was [also] missing, ripped from its place in the cue-sheet notebook."

According to Smith, "The lighting engineer and dancers carried on in an improvised fashion. It was only the experience and cleverness of the dancers and the lighting engineer that allowed the scene to succeed with very little sacrifice of artistic quality."

He continued, "During the dance numbers on the stage, the dressing room area was locked, owing to the possibility that dancers would defect. Also, personal valuables and expensive costumes were kept in the dressing room complex. After the final scene, the 30 dancers trooped into the dressing room area to shed their outfits. As they approached dressing room 8, the dancers were stunned by what they saw. The missing dagger was embedded in the door to the dressing room, and page 13 of the lighting cue sheet was impaled on the point of the knife."

Smith acknowledged that "for months afterward, conjecture abounded as to the significance of the event. There was never any question that it was the work of Shorty. Whether or not the presence of a foreign dance troupe or the lamentable existence of the Cold War prompted the action of Shorty is not known."

A few years after the occurrence, Shorty was once again at work—this time with the theater's lights.

"In 1985, a solo opera singer was scheduled to appear at the Capitol Theatre," Smith said. "Her performance was a medley of popular arias. The only other person on stage with the star was the musician accompanying her on the piano. The stage lights above bathed the singer in a soft blue wash. In addition to overhead stage lights, theaters traditionally use powerful spotlights to accent the performers. Spotlights form a brightly defined circle that follows the performer across the stage."

He continued, "The opera singer gave a sterling performance and was awarded with a standing ovation. When the curtain came down, the singer was quick to thank the stagehands for their diligence and competency. She especially singled out the work of the spotlight operators, praising their smoothness and on-target work as the best she had ever experienced. The stage manager was speechless. In a perplexed voice, he told the opera singer that the two spotlight operators had both called in sick with food poisoning. There had been nobody in the spot booth operating the lights during the show."

Shorty is also often credited with turning the stage lights on at times when employees were close enough to the lighting console to see that no one had touched it.

No one visible to human eyes, that is. But when Shorty made spotlights dance about the stage in a ballet-like sequence, Roger Smith decided it was time for him to take action. As quickly and quietly as he could, the stage manager made his way up the stairs to the catwalks where the lights are hung. When he found footprints but nothing else, he knew that the light-dance hadn't been the work of a practical joker at all. It was simply another demonstration of Shorty's powers of illumination.

It's generally believed that, when he was alive, Shorty was somehow involved with the technical aspects of the theater. But the ghost has a non-technical, more playful side too, such as when he opened the grand stage curtain. Smith also recounted that "at the conclusion of a show, ushers routinely put all of the 1500 seats in the upright position. It has been reported at least twice that the janitor has entered the theater a few hours later and found all 1500 seats in the down position."

Shorty apparently has a ghostly aversion to rock and roll and so, when the Capitol Theatre hosts such a musical event, the staff have to be extra vigilant to ensure a successful show.

The ghost has also performed at least one super-human, lifesaving feat. When a piece of equipment above the stage broke away and began to fall, it was on a direct path to a woman standing on stage. The object was heavy and, had it landed where it was headed, the woman would almost certainly have been killed. As another employee at the theater watched in horror, unable to do anything, the projectile impossibly changed course in mid-fall, likely averting a tragedy.

This heroic spirit is not above displaying some very human failings. When staff leave a plate of cookies out overnight, the plate is always empty in the morning.

Over the years, changes to the structure of the theater have made one door completely inaccessible, among other things. It's located 12 feet (about 4 meters) above the backstage area and is never used. No one currently with the theater knows whether it leads to a room or perhaps only to a blank wall. The staff calls it "Shorty's door" because, even though no one (living) ever goes near it, the door occasionally stands open. Psychics investigating the theater found a phantom heat source near the door—a source well above the floor.

Management at the Capitol Theatre has no interest in trying to operate without their invisible helper. When a pair of "ghost hunters" asked to tour the haunted old theater, management agreed but only if they promised not to exorcise Shorty.

Despite the staff's fondness for their ghost, very few people are comfortable with being alone in the enormous old building.

Lone staff members have reported unexplained noises during late night shifts in the massive theatre—"footsteps in deserted hallways, clanging in the ventilation shafts, the elevator running and no one on board," Roger informed me. "No staff member opts to be in the Capitol Theatre alone after midnight." Although the fears may not be justified, Roger believes that adherence to the old adage "better safe than sorry" keeps everyone happy.

By now, Shorty and the Capitol Theatre are clearly inseparable. As Roger Smith concluded, "The Capitol

Theatre is a unique building. It is special in that it is on the National Register of Historic Buildings. It is also extraordinary in that it possesses an invisible caretaker. An invisible entity. A ghost."

A ghost simply named "Shorty."

Samuel and his Friends

After only 14 years of operation, the once-glorious Winter Garden Theatre in downtown Toronto stood dark—and deserted—for more than 65 years. By 1981, demolition seemed inevitable until the Ontario Heritage Foundation intervened. When workers from the foundation reopened the theater to begin their enormous renovation and preservation project, they walked into a time capsule. The cavernous old hall stood as it had after hosting its final performance in 1928. Here, the seemingly impossible had happened—time had eerily stood still. Original vaudeville scenery remained where it was last used, performers' notes were found pinned to walls in dressing rooms. Old ticket stubs lay where they been dropped by patrons, many no doubt long dead. The surreal surroundings, disrupted only by the occasional pigeon fluttering about, appeared to be about as empty and lifeless as a place could be.

Once renovations got under way, the Winter Garden Theatre suddenly didn't seem to be empty at all. Right from the beginning, groups of energetic and enthusiastic volunteer workers began to note "strange goings-on," according to Alison Truelove of the Ontario Heritage Foundation.

The spirits in the Winter Garden Theatre are content to spend their afterlives in this splendid building.

On more than one occasion, as workers stood and watched, a row of spring-loaded seats would fold down as though a group of people had just seated themselves to watch a show. The seat bottoms would remain down for a time and then, in unison, fold up against the chair backs as though those same unseen people had risen and left after enjoying a performance.

A group of curious volunteers took a Ouija board into the theater. Their initiative was rewarded immediately as "Samuel" identified himself to them. Through the board, Samuel explained that he had been a trombone player in a 1918 vaudeville production at the Winter Garden. Presumably he'd enjoyed his tenure at the then-fashionable hall and had returned to it in death, perhaps hoping to spend a peaceful eternity surrounded by the theatre's silent splendor.

Because so many of the volunteers had witnessed the eerie phenomenon of seats folding down for no apparent reason, they were convinced that, as forthcoming as Samuel might be, he was not the only presence in the place. They asked the spirit of the trombone player if he was alone or if there were, indeed, other entities in the hall.

Yes, there were others, many others, confirmed Samuel. "May we speak with some of them?" the inquisitive group probed. "No" came Samuel's unarguable response. It seemed the long-dead musician was enjoying being in the limelight once again, for he steadfastly refused to let the living people communicate with any of the other ghosts in the building.

Although no one's been able to "talk" to any of the other ethereal residents of the Winter Garden Theatre, those silent spirits have managed to make their presences known just the same.

"There are three elevators in the building," Alison Truelove explained. "They are all hand operated from the inside so technically they cannot go anywhere unless someone is in them. Despite this, after one elevator is used it doesn't stay at that floor, but always returns to a particular floor."

As well, theater patrons have reported seeing a woman dressed in Edwardian clothing in the lobby. She appears only fleetingly and is gone by the time the patrons realize that what they are seeing is highly irregular and either look again or try to draw a companion's attention to the unusual image.

And so at the Winter Garden Theatre the living and the dead peacefully coexist. Neither Samuel nor any of his supernatural colleagues have ever been threatening. They seem to have remained behind, refreshingly unaware of time as we perceive it, perhaps enjoying the glorious new life that the living have breathed into the resurrected hall.

Judy, Judy, Judy

Judy is the primary ghost in Bellingham, Washington's Mount Baker Theatre. She's certainly not the only spirit present, though. When members of a camera crew from a local television show brought a psychic into the theater, the sensitive woman "said that there was…a troupe of ghosts in the theater," explained house manager Anna Marie. "They are down on the main stage, stage left, front and downstage. They're just kind of hanging out with us."

Judy's devotion to the theater is especially gratifying as, in life, she was not really connected with the stage in any way. She is thought to be the ghost of a woman who lived in a house that once stood where the theater does now. Legend has it the woman was killed when the house burned to the ground more than 70 years ago. Judy's not a shy spirit. Former house manager Margaret Mackay had an unforgettable firsthand encounter with Judy. As Margaret walked through the lobby, she was hit by an "incredibly cold blast of air that seemed to move right through" her. The woman paused in surprise. As she did, the lights in the theater flickered.

Although Judy is usually invisible, she may have allowed herself to be photographed once. Margaret Mackay snapped a picture in one of the theater's hallways. When the film was developed, that frame displayed an image of a strange mist or vapor—the kind of disturbance in the air that is so often associated with an entity's presence.

While staff at the Mount Baker Theatre are justifiably pleased that they have a picture of at least one of their resident phantoms, they're likely far more delighted that everyone involved with the theater—dead and alive—seems able to work together in harmony.

SCENE V

Terriss and the Adelphi

Mid-December 1897. Behind the scenes at the Adelphi Theatre on the Strand in London, England, the stage was being set for a tragedy.

Richard Archer Prince was a disgruntled and unsuccessful actor. He was completely—although inaccurately—convinced that the blame for his stalled career could be placed squarely on the shoulders of someone else. Sadly a handful of Prince's co-workers thought it great sport to reinforce the paranoid man's delusions. Passing themselves off as his friends, they assured Prince that his fears were justified, that it was only leading man William Terriss' fear of losing center stage that kept Prince from being awarded starring roles. Behind Prince's back, however, they called him the "Mad Archer" and were most gratified and amused to see how their comments fed the man's self-deception.

Terriss was blissfully unaware of both the second-rate actor's growing rage and the vicious teasing that was stoking it. In fact, there was little in life that concerned William Terriss. He seemed to have it all—good looks, a fulfilling stage career, countless adoring fans and, for the most part, co-workers who respected him.

One of those respectful co-workers was fellow actor Frederick Lane, Terriss' understudy for the production of the melodrama *Secret Service.* On the afternoon of Thursday, December 16, 1897, Lane rushed to get to the theater. Like most actors, he went to bed relatively late and slept away most of his mornings. This particular day was different—terribly different—because he had been jolted awake by a gruesome and graphic nightmare. He had dreamed that his mentor, Terriss, had been murdered. In his sleep Lane had seen Terriss' body in a heap on the stairs near the dressing rooms, his open shirt revealing a fatal stab wound.

Lane tried in vain to convince others at the theater that his dream had been an important omen. Perhaps not wanting to believe that Terriss' safety might really be in jeopardy, those he talked to were unconvinced They laughed at Lane, suggesting that a stop at the local pub, not insight, had caused his nightmare.

Sadly, Lane's premonition was accurate. That evening, when Terriss arrived at the theater's stage door for the evening performance, a cloaked figure jumped out from the shadows of Maiden Lane and plunged a dagger into his chest. The sound of the victim's body collapsing against the door brought the other members of the cast running. They carried Terriss' bleeding body into the theater and crowded about him while he spoke his last words.

"I will come back."

As Terriss took his last breath, Seymour Hicks, who some months later married the dying actor's daughter, heard a disembodied voice demand, "Are men such fools as to think there is no hereafter?" William Terriss was dead, murdered.

Police had little difficulty arresting the guilty man. The "Mad Archer" had made no attempt to flee the scene of his crime. In due course, he was convicted of murder and sentenced to spend the rest of his days in custody at the Broadmoor Criminal Lunatic Asylum. The man's physical health was clearly much stronger than his mental health: Prince lived until 1937, dying at the age of 81—9 years after the spirit of William Terriss first appeared, making good on his promise to "come back."

The initial appearance of the ghost was not immediately recognized for what it undoubtedly was. A comedic actress resting between performances was disturbed when the cot she was lying on suddenly shook. This unexplained movement was followed by a distinct series of raps on her dressing room door. When she opened the door, she found the hallway empty. It wasn't until an employee familiar with the history of the theater arrived at work that the reasons for the woman's odd experiences were made clear. It seemed the dressing room she'd been assigned was the same one that William Terriss' female co-star, Jessie Milward, routinely used. Terriss always gave a particular pattern of raps on the door as he passed by to let her know when he'd arrived at the theater.

Since that time, the apparition, dressed in his signature frock coat and top hat, has been seen retracing the actor's usual route into the theater before vanishing through a closed and locked dressing room door. Maintenance men and other workers have reported seeing the long-deceased star's image in various parts of the theater—strolling unaffectedly through an otherwise empty lobby or discreetly observing a production from the wings. The manifestation seems unaware of his present surroundings and does not respond to any of the astonished people who've seen him.

Activities at the Adelphi are consistent with the common patterns of a truly haunted "house." The lights turn on and off when no one's near them, phantom lights are occasionally seen in one or more of the actors' dressing rooms and there are unexplainable, localized pockets of cold air about the place. An empty elevator in the theater will operate in a purposeful fashion although no one is near it—no one visible, that is. Many actresses have been awakened from pre-show naps in their dressing rooms by an unseen force moving the couches they recline on.

Phantom footsteps and knocks on walls in empty hallways have become so common that those who know the theater barely give the ghostly sounds a second thought. Perhaps the strangest aspect of the William Terriss ghost story is how well traveled the image is, for he is also seen late at night in the local underground station. In life, it was Terriss' habit to catch the last subway train home, and apparently he's still commuting to some unknown place or plane.

In the past decade, this spirit may have had another specter join him. A psychic touring the theater spoke with great conviction about the presence of a female dancer throughout the auditorium. The manifestation was extremely happy, wanting only to be left alone to dance away her eternity.

It would certainly be fascinating to know whether or not there is any "otherworldly" communication between the two spirits.

Kate, Ghost of the Klondike

During the late 1800s and early 1900s financial fortunes were made and lost—and then made again—often to be lost a second or even a third or fourth time. "Robber barons," wheelers and dealers with nerves of steel, dominated the international economy, and many business dealings were corrupt. Alexander Pantages fit in well with those high rollers. Perhaps to his credit, Pantages' success had a longer run than that of some others.

Born into a destitute family in Greece, Pantages began his journey to his eventual theater empire in 1878 when, as a child of seven, he stowed away on a ship bound for South America. Some 20 years later, after working at myriad jobs, Pantages joined the hundreds of thousands of would-be millionaires trekking north in search of gold. By the time he reached Dawson City in the Yukon, Pantages had managed to lose the money he would have needed to stake a claim if he'd found one worthy of staking.

Apparently unfazed by his loss, the 26-year-old simply started from nothing again. He took a job as a waiter, which lasted only until he'd won the heart of a beautiful young lady. Kathleen Eloisa Rockwell had been a chorus girl in New York before the excitement of the gold rush lured her north. Miss Rockwell became an enormously popular and successful singer and dancer in Dawson City. "The Belle of the Yukon" some called her. Others referred to her as "Klondike Kate."

The handsome Pantages wasted no time in charming Klondike Kate into investing her money in a theater he wanted to open. All went well for a time. With the combination of Kate's capital and Pantages' eye for detail, the Orpheum Theatre prospered. Although he had no background in the arts, the entrepreneur was wise enough to listen and respond to his audiences. (He also swept the theater floor each night, not so much because he liked cleanliness but so that he could pocket any gold nuggets dropped by members of the audience.)

Soon Pantages became so wealthy that he apparently felt it was safe to leave the north (and the woman who had bankrolled his success) for the potential excitement and milder climate of Seattle. There he opened another theater—the first to be named the Pantages. The man's business empire grew until his namesake chain of theaters dotted North America.

Unfortunately, he didn't foresee that the novelty known as "movies" would replace live entertainment, and by the 1920s his box office receipts had begun to wane. He sold off most of his holdings in 1927, and for a time the new owners kept the Pantages name on the marquees. In 1928, however, Alexander Pantages was charged with a serious crime. The accusations were never proven, but his name had been effectively tarnished; all the Pantages theaters in Canada were subsequently renamed. He died in obscurity with few people of the following generations even knowing his name, let alone the important role he once played in the entertainment industry.

And what became of the jilted Klondike Kate? The poor woman never recovered from the heartbreak of having been cast aside by the man she had loved and supported. Despite her never-ending sorrow, Kate lived to the age of 80, dying in 1957. In death, her spirit returned to haunt the theater she'd originally financed.

By the early 1960s, the building that had brought both wealth and sorrow to its founders was in dangerously bad disrepair. The theater was torn down and, as a tourist attraction, it was replaced with an exact replica. The ghost of Klondike Kate, perhaps oblivious to all that was going on around her spirit, remained at the site throughout the demolition and reconstruction.

Painters and carpenters working on the new theater reported seeing what they described as "a very pretty lady" on the stage. The image seemed to stare at the workers for a few moments before "disappearing into thin air."

After construction of the new facility was completed, Parks Canada began running tours of the theater and at least one guide, Jane Olynyk, was aware of the ghost's lingering presence. On a Monday night in August 1976, Jane was locking the place up for the night. Part of that routine involved making sure that no one had stayed behind in any of the theater's seats. Toward this end, Jane made her way to center stage after turning on the "house lights" to illuminate the auditorium. That was when she saw Kate's apparition. The ghost wasn't menacing; she was simply there, standing on the left side of the second balcony.

The sighting didn't frighten Jane, who knew the folklore about the ghost and even recognized the apparition from archival photographs she'd seen of Klondike Kate. If the ghost's flamboyant gown and distinctive red hair weren't enough proof of the haunting, the fact that the image was ever-so-slightly transparent certainly would have been.

Moments later, the manifestation began to walk away. It looked back, smiled down at Jane, and then vanished. The sensitive and accepting tour guide felt warmed by that initial encounter, but after subsequent visits she could feel the deceased woman's great sorrow. This sensation, Jane reported, was an all-encompassing one that she could not help being affected by.

Although not everyone is as sensitive to the ghost as Jane was, Kate's spirit is widely accepted as an important part of the theater. Most people associated with the place feel that her specter is a guardian of sorts and enjoy her continuing presence.

And so, in an odd way, the legacy of Alexander Pantages and the theaters he owned lives on—in death perhaps forever.

An Extra Chill in the Air

Janet Hewlett-Davies, now a representative of the Little Theatre Guild at Brighton's New Venture Theatre in England, wrote to let me know of her encounter with a ghost in another theater.

Janet began her retelling by setting the stage: "In the 1960s, I was a member of the Crescent Theatre, Birmingham, then in its original 18th-century home. On a winter's Sunday evening, I arrived at the empty theater to arrange things for a performance of a poetry reading I produced. I rang the bell beside the stage door to attract George, the caretaker, who lived in a flat above the theater.

"There was no sign of George, but then I realized that the stage door was unlocked and I went into the theater. I put on the backstage lights and made my way toward the front of the house to start the preliminary arrangements. This entailed walking through the scene-dock and through a pass-door into the foyer, where a fire had been laid in the hearth. I lit the fire, but was unable to turn on any lights because all front-of-house lights were operated by key, not switch, and I did not have the necessary key."

Having described her surroundings very effectively, Hewlett-Davies added an important detail about herself. She confirmed, "I am not afraid of the dark, and the light from the fire gave me some illumination as I made my way down the corridor to the front-of-house kitchen to switch on stoves and kettles for the refreshments that were part of the entertainment.

"Halfway down the corridor, I stopped, unable to go any farther. I was not afraid, but I knew there was something dreadful beyond the point where I had stopped. Nothing could have persuaded me to go beyond there.

"At that moment, the lights snapped on and George, light-key in hand, stood just a few yards away with an odd expression on his face. He asked if anything was wrong—asked in a way that made me think he already knew the answer.

"I told him what had happened, and George looked at the ceiling above the point where I had stopped. He said, 'That's where he did it.' 'Did what?' I asked."

It was then that the woman first learned the haunted history of the Crescent Theatre. She explained, "George told me the story, which probably lots of other people in the theater knew but which had never reached me. The [building] had started its life as a public hall, the Baskerville Hall. It was a spacious building and, early in the 19th century, the caretaker of the day had made extra money by using the upper rooms to run an informal but very successful brothel."

The janitor's extracurricular activities came to an end when, "on a Sunday evening," the local constabulary was informed of his money-making operation. When he saw the police approaching the hall, the man must have panicked, for "they arrived to find him hanging, framed in the window and silhouetted by the firelight behind him."

But what did this suicide, on another Sunday night 40 years before, have to do with Janet Hewlett-Davies' strong and strange reaction?

"George took me outside and showed me that window. I realized that it was, indeed, directly above the point in the corridor where I had stopped."

The restless spirit from the man's suicide had remained in the theater, scarring the psychic landscape so sufficiently that, all those years later, Janet Hewlett-Davies was able to sense the strong, negative force even though she initially had no idea what it was she was reacting to.

SCENE VIII

George Street: Its Ghost, Its Theater

At 54 George Street in Edinburgh, Scotland, you'll find a theater, often called the Assembly Rooms. It is used by the Third Stage Production Company, among others. Nestled between Princes and Thistle streets, George Street is also home to Jane's ghost. Her apparition is a most dramatic sighting. Although her image is solid, witnesses usually realize immediately that they are staring at a ghost, for her impeccable clothing is years and years out of date. She wears white gloves and a small white hat with two plumes—one white to match the hat, the other blue to match her coat. As understated as her clothing is, Jane's ghost makes an overstatement when it comes to her jewelry, a dizzying array of pendants, bracelets, buckles and bangles.

If, as you're passing the theater and the sight of her ghost isn't enough to convince you that you've just had a paranormal encounter, then perhaps the deep chill you feel emanating from her aura should. Despite these signs, it seems that not everyone is aware of her presence, because witnesses who have seen Jane clearly have observed that those around them do not seem to see the same sight.

Jane's image has also been seen on a very rainy day walking along George Street by the theater. That time, the ghost was very easy to recognize for what she was: while people all around her wore raincoats and were wet and muddy, Jane glided along the sidewalk oblivious to it all— as dry and clean as could be. Clearly it was not raining on her plane. Although few people seemed to notice her presence, a horse, hitched to a rather regal-looking cart, whinnied as she passed.

Research indicates that the phantom's proximity to the theater itself is somewhat coincidental. In life the young woman's name was Jane Vernelt. Apparently she preferred to call herself Mademoiselle Vernelt. She had owned a clothing business near the George Street theater, but had been advised to sell it because of her mental instability. The actual transfer of the business to the new owners was more than poor Jane could bear.

At that point, this ghost story becomes one of those rare cases of a soul being seen before the physical body has actually deceased. While Jane Vernelt's physical body was still alive and confined to restraints, her image was often seen near the theater on George Street, strolling past the shop she'd so proudly owned for so many years. Death alone was not enough to stop her soul and, even after her death in 1893, she was regularly seen enjoying herself as she wandered along her favorite route.

There have been no reports of Jane's image for many years now, and it's presumed that she's finally gone to her eternal rest. Or perhaps she's just slipped into the theater at 54 George Street and is enjoying the entertainment provided therein.

SCENE IX

Musical Manifestation

The Avon Theater in Utica, New York, slightly southwest of the Adirondack Mountains, was demolished in 1947. When it was torn down, the once-grand old theater took its secrets with it. One of those secrets was whether or not the place had ever been haunted. If, in fact, the theater wasn't home to a ghost, then someone (an electrician is the most frequently named suspect) evidently perpetrated a successful hoax.

The story goes that, early in the 20th century, a woman brandishing a gun ran down the center aisle of the auditorium. When she reached the orchestra pit, she fired the weapon at the organist, killing him instantly. Apparently the victim and his assassin had been man and wife at the time. Their disagreement revolved around the issue of his marital infidelity. The woman clearly preferred to be widowed than cheated upon, so the organist's punishment for his adultery was death.

Ghostly activity began almost immediately after the murder, and it reached such a pitch that the theater owners had difficulty keeping employees. On one occasion, security guards on the night shift listened in horror as ominous music filled the theater. They ran into the auditorium to investigate but the sounds stopped immediately upon their entrance. They discovered that the organ was no longer beneath the stage in the orchestra pit where it belonged when no one was playing it, but had instead been elevated to a height parallel to the stage.

The building has been gone for more than 50 years, so we cannot know for certain if the ghostly events were a clever hoax or if the ghost of the murdered man was returning at night to finish playing the tune his wronged wife so effectively interrupted.

THE
HAUNTED STAGE

Ghosts by the Dozens

Some types of buildings seem more prone to attracting (and keeping) ghosts than others. The very existence of this book provides evidence that theaters are one such easily haunted venue, but there are others. Firehalls, hotels and schools quickly come to mind. And when a building has served as a schoolhouse before becoming a theater, resident ghosts are almost inevitable.

The experiences of J.T. Smith with his Old Schoolhouse Theater on Sanibel Island, just off the west coast of Florida, emphatically confirm this theory.

"WE HAVE 56 GHOSTS!" Smith exclaimed, before explaining, "Our ghosts don't all appear at once, but at different times. They are [the souls of] performers and other persons associated with our 95-seat theater over the past 33 years."

J.T. has been able to identify some of the spirits. For instance, he states with conviction, "Ruth and Philip Hunter, the theater's first producers and performers, have inhabited the theater since their deaths."

Those presences J.T. recognized and welcomed right from the start, but when a local newspaper asked if they could do a Halloween feature on the haunted building and bring along a psychic, J.T. found that there were far more than just those two ghosts in the place.

"The psychic could hear school children playing in the back and saw a young woman named Annabelle who scurries about picking up after everyone," he recalled. He then added that he found that particular ghost especially intriguing because "the most common ghostly occurrence is the disappearance of things or finding items where you know you didn't leave them."

J.T. continued, "The psychic noted that the spirits were all friendly and were here because they had happy memories in and of the building. Many actors inhabit the theater because they are unable to 'go to the light,' so they've settled where they are most comfortable. They like the energy of the building and the positive energy from the audience and performers during the shows."

Some of the resident phantoms may even have inspired creativity on occasion. "When my past associate, Ken Loewit, and I would reach a creative lull, we would sit in the empty [theater] quietly and the ideas would begin to flow. Who knows if the spirits had anything to do with this, but I would like to think so."

The owner of this quaint theater welcomes the resident ghosts.

Given the sheer numbers of specters roaming about the place, J.T.'s assumption seems fair. All that positive spectral energy floating about is bound to produce a positive outcome of some kind.

The man also remembers being at a meeting a few years ago in the front office. The discussion was going well until those convened were interrupted by the sounds of someone running a finger along the keyboard of the piano. There is a piano in the theater but at that particular moment no one was near it. No one that anyone could see, that is.

Although J.T. certainly doesn't take a ghostly roll call every day, he's very much aware that Annabelle, at least, is still in residence. Much to his good-natured chagrin, he notes that around the haunted theater "many things disappear—frequently." That's not too surprising, considering the history of the building.

SCENE II

School Spirit

When collecting ghost stories for this book, I began by placing inquiries in newsletters that circulate among theater personnel. Two of the replies I received came from Georgia. Oddly, both stories are connected with college theaters located many miles apart.

A gentleman who gave his name only as "Brown" wrote about an experience he had late one night in the spring of 1996, while he was working alone in the box office of the Berry College Theatre Company. Brown explained that Mount Berry, the town the college is in, is roughly an hour's drive northwest of Atlanta.

Brown also explained that the theater building is over 100 years old and has served many purposes over time. With such a history, there has been more than sufficient opportunity for the building to become haunted. From details provided by Brown, it sounds as though that is exactly what has happened.

Brown, who described himself as "a fairly skeptical individual," began describing his encounter by noting that, "It was the middle of the night. I was all alone in the box office of our theater working on copy for an approaching deadline. The doors were locked, the alarms were set, I was sure I had plenty of time to work in solitude."

After working in silence for some time, Brown was most surprised to hear laughter coming from "near the stage area. Without a doubt, I know I heard laughter. It was real melodramatic and campy."

The laughter sounded so real that the man presumed somebody was really there and had found his or her own unauthorized presence in a locked, secured building highly amusing.

Brown continued, "I'm kind of a skinny guy. It's doubtful that I would have been able to physically detain an intruder, so I decided to respond to the obnoxious laughter by snickering, to sort of mock the laughing intruder, and as a measure of pure frolic. So I laughed, but then the [phantom] laughing stopped."

Now the man was even more disconcerted. "*Humpf,* I thought. And I thought. And I thought. And I thought. And my heart began to beat a little faster at the general creepiness of the whole event. I'd obviously gotten the attention of who or whatever it was that felt the need to chuckle with such hearty fervor."

Judging by what happened next, the man had great justification for holding that opinion, for "the same minute, a 'presence' came into the box office and approached me. Mind you, I was facing my computer screen, just as I am while I am writing this; thus, eye contact was never made. And no, for heaven's sake, I did not turn around on my swiveling stool to meet this merry whatever it was. However, I swear to you that I sensed a presence, just as one would be aware if there was someone else standing, sitting or floating directly behind him or her. It stayed for a full minute or so. There was definitely a presence that lingered behind me, encompassed in some sort of an energy source—a positive energy source."

How could Brown have been so very sure—aside from his decidedly conclusive feelings, that is? He continued, "A reflection of hovering bright light, which I clearly saw on my computer monitor screen, was confirmation enough."

It's highly unlikely that Brown is as comfortably skeptical today as he was the day before that supernatural encounter.

· · ·

Jennifer Jenkins from DeKalb College in the Atlanta suburb of Clarkston wrote about a haunting that began in their school's theater in 1982.

"The college was hosting a dance company's annual performance," Jennifer began. "In the middle of the program, the dancers were performing to a lively piece of music by Carl Orff. Everything had been running quite smoothly when, simultaneously, the lights started to flicker and the reel-to-reel tape 'stuttered,' dragged, then speeded up. All of this was over [seemingly] as quickly as it had begun. The well-trained dancers continued the performance and picked up the beat flawlessly once the music was restored to correct 'pitch.' "

The dancers may have recovered quickly, but the technicians weren't quite as calm. Jennifer explained that even after their initial "adrenaline rush, they could not assess why this mysterious sequence had happened. There had not been a power 'brownout' anywhere else in the building and it never happened again—that night."

The event remained a mystery until it was learned that Carl Orff, the composer whose music was being played during the strange occurrence, had died on "that very night" in 1982. Could his soul have been attracted to the college stage by the strains of his own composition? It would seem so.

"Ever since that night, whenever we have had an unexplainable 'glitch' in the light or sound [systems] we blame Carl." Jennifer added, "We have noticed a sharp decrease in incidents after posting several pictures of Carl Orff in the [technical] booth."

Jennifer may have found an effective method of tapping into some otherworldly assistance. She explained, "I have been known to hum a few measures of *Carmina Burana* [one of Orff's most celebrated works] when things don't seem to be going well. It seems to help."

Mary and the Orpheum

Lively debate revolves around whether she died in 1921, 1923 or 1928. Conflicting opinions exist about how she died. Was it in a fire? A motor vehicle accident? Or a mishap that involved her falling to her death? There seems to be little doubt, however, that Mary is the ghost in Memphis, Tennessee's extravagant Orpheum Theatre.

Pat Halloran, manager of the Orpheum, is the man who wrote the book about the theater. "I wrote the history of the theater except the part about the ghost. I had someone else write that section because I'm a skeptic." Admirably, despite his stance, Mr. Halloran strongly upholds the story's right to be included as a piece of the building's legendary background.

The theater on South Main Street in Memphis first opened in 1890 but the original building burned to the ground in 1923. The Orpheum was reconstructed and, in 1928, the palatial auditorium reopened. It's not known exactly when Mary's ghost was first noticed, but that initial sighting must have occurred in the newer building because all those who saw the spirit presumed that she had lost her life in the blaze.

Some time later some parapsychology students from Memphis State University held a séance in the theater under the supervision of their professor, Dr. Lee Sutter. The entity was able to explain why she's haunting the theater and when and how she arrived. Mary's soul informed the group that in 1928, she had been hit by a trolley bus traveling along South Main Street. She was immediately taken into the Orpheum for medical attention but, sadly, all attempts to save the girl's life were in vain. Her injuries were fatal and she died just moments later. A popular legend indicates that her spirit has never left the place.

Mary's ghostly image is unchanging. She's consistently described as a little girl, estimated to be about 12 years of age. She has brown hair, which is always tied into pigtails. The dress (or smock, as some have referred to it) the little wraith wears is so white it actually seems to glow and, although she moves with a gliding motion, her footsteps can occasionally be heard, especially as she makes her way to "her" seat—c-5.

In predictable ghostly fashion, Mary causes doors to swing open and closed again, at times when no one (visible) is near that door. When lights in the various parts of the building flicker, the staff members know that Mary's mischievous little self is nearby and seeking attention. While those tricks of the ghostly realm may be really quite ordinary, and even expected in a haunted building, one of her most annoying stunts was unique. She placed workers' tools into toilets!

On another occasion, in the early 1960s, a man named Harlan Judkins, in company with his brother and a mutual friend, began some necessary repair work on the Orpheum's grand old pipe organ. He had never heard any of the ghost lore surrounding the theater and, despite his strange experiences, still urges skepticism. He is quite detailed and forthcoming in describing his encounters, presumably with Mary. The three men were laboring away

The lavish Orpheum Theatre, home to the ghost of a young girl.

late into the night when they came across a particularly difficult problem with the organ. They left the building and went across the street to a restaurant for a coffee break. A short time later, the men returned to the theater where they discovered that the problem, which minutes before had them stumped, was "somehow fixed."

As they puzzled over this bizarre development, the temperature in the theater dropped dramatically and they all felt a presence join them. "Who's there?" they called out, but no one answered. The men immediately packed their tools away and left the building.

Judkins had to go back into the theater another night—this time by himself. He conceded that the encounter he had on that second evening was subtle but also admitted that it had left him decidedly "unnerved." According to the write-up in the book about the theater's history, on this solo occasion Harlan Judkins held a set of electrical wires in his hand. They were "all correctly bundled." To his annoyance, the man then realized that he needed his screwdriver. It was nearby on the floor, but just out of reach. He was loath to put the cluster of wires down because rebundling them would've been a very time-consuming chore. As he debated his options, Judkins looked down at the floor again. The screwdriver was still there, but this time the tool was lying right at his feet.

With great justification, the man later said of the incident, "I don't want to understand this," and he reported that he left the theater as soon as he could after that helpful, but definitely enigmatic, event had occurred.

For the cast in the Orpheum's 1977 production of *Fiddler on the Roof*, sightings of the ghost's image actually became routine, and although details of the scare Mary gave actor Yul Brynner in 1982 have been lost, he was definitely "spooked." Little wonder; Mary likes to have things her way.

Organist Vincent Astor, who has also served as the general manager of the Orpheum, noted that it is safer not to use the ghost's name and one should never, "under any circumstances, make fun of her." Why? "She's been known to retaliate." Despite that warning, Astor also acknowledged, "She is a very good ghost."

In April 1979, when Vincent Astor was performing an organ concert for a group who had stayed behind at the theater, Mary put on quite a show of ghostly activity. Teresa Spoone was among those gathered and she recalled that the auditorium became "deathly cold" whenever Astor played the song "Never, Never Land." The implication is that the musician played that piece more than once during the evening. That may seem strange until you realize that "Never, Never Land" is from the musical *Peter*

Pan, a story about a magical, "supernatural" place with equally extraordinary people in it. You could question whether Astor was entirely in charge of his playlist for that concert or whether some more mystical force was at work with him.

Be that as it may, Spoone also reported that later that evening she felt "scared" and that she "knew something was out there…it was an overpowering feeling."

Spoone took a quick glance into what seemed to be the affected area. Her suspicions were confirmed—there stood an image of a little girl. Feeling that she was acting against her own will, Spoone proceeded to go toward the apparition. "It was like she was calling me," the woman described, and added that she stopped walking toward the ghost because she felt it was extremely dangerous, that "I'd never come back the same."

Two others in the group rushed toward Mary's figure, but by then the ghost could no longer be seen. Just at that moment, the door to a nearby broom closet began rattling as though someone was trying to get in or out of it. When the rattling noise stopped, the ghost reappeared. The ghostly activity lasted for the entire evening, and Mary's apparition is estimated to have remained visible for an extraordinarily long three-quarters of an hour.

For years, management at the Orpheum Theatre declined to acknowledge any of the ghost stories associated with the place. Fortunately for Mary, and for those of us who love ghost stories, this situation is no longer the case. The official stance now at this gorgeous hall in Memphis is that it accepts the ethereal extra as another wonderful part of its fascinating past, present and future.

Devotion Survives Death

"When does Gilmor Brown get any time for his personal life?" a concerned observer once asked the thespian. The answer, from a colleague and close friend of Gilmor's, was "His life *is* the theater." Today, more than 40 years after his passing, it would seem that the theater has remained his principal preoccupation. He loved his art so much that even an imposition as inconvenient as death has not been able to weaken the former impresario's commitment to the Pasadena Playhouse, a theater he helped to create in 1925.

For the next 35 years, the playhouse attracted stars to its stage and crowds to its seats. And Gilmor continued to be a busy, satisfied and respected member of the California theater community. In 1960, at the age of 74, Gilmor Brown's life on earth ended. Sadly, the playhouse that he worked so hard to build soon fell into disrepair. By 1969, when the theater closed its doors, it was a shabby travesty of the splendid hall that, in 1937, the State of California Legislature had unanimously given the honorary designation of "State Theater."

The edifice stood eerily empty for 10 years before work began to restore the once-beautiful building to its former glory. When the theater reopened the following year, it was an occasion that Peter Parkin, currently the president of the Pasadena Playhouse Alumni and Associates, remembers well. In his role as technical director, Parkin says he was responsible for "re-wiring the…theatre and building the set."

Gilmor Brown served the Pasadena Playhouse even after his death.

The age-old dilemma of too much work and too few available hands meant that Peter was a very busy man during those weeks. He was building sets in the theater's shop and then dragging them down a hallway into the theater itself. The process was exhausting, but the work had to get done. He explained that one night he'd been "working by myself. I got very tired by around 11:00. Usually I would lock up [then] and go home, but this night I had finished all the platforms and decided to surprise the cast and crew by having the set in place for the next rehearsal. I started dragging the platforms, which were ¾" plywood framed with two-by-fours, down the long hallway in the gloom of only a couple of 100-watt bulbs dangling from the ceiling. The place was spooky during the day, but at night and alone…"

Peter let his sentence trail off since the implication was clear—solitary work at night in the playhouse was a very eerie situation. Worse, the hours of heavy work had taken their toll on the well-intentioned worker. He was tired—or, as he described it, his "fanny [was] severely dragging"—and despite the motivation of his self-imposed challenge, the man was ready to give up and head for home. And that was when Gilmor may have stepped up to offer some much-needed but ghostly assistance. As Parkin struggled with the next platform, he suddenly felt it "kind of take off on me." It seemed as though there was someone at the other end pushing the heavy wooden set toward Peter as he was attempting to pull it.

But if the helper was in fact Gilmor, the ghost's efforts were neither immediately helpful nor appreciated, for the usually calm technical director stated, "I freaked out...dropped the platforms and headed outside through the nearest door. Had there not been a door nearby, I probably would have made one. I was so frightened. The place had been very spooky and I was not comfortable there, especially by myself."

Once safely out of the theater, Peter's practical side came to the fore. "Finally, I decided that I was a rational human being...that there was no such thing as a ghost...[that] I was tired and, what the heck, it was sure...easier to move those darn platforms now. I went back inside and went to work."

Peter's initial reaction of fright proved nothing more than a fear of the unknown, for he went on to explain that the encounter soon became a positive one. "Once I relaxed with it, I actually started to have fun. [F]rom that moment on, the atmosphere in the building changed for me. It went from cold and scary to friendly and warm."

Today there is no question in Peter Parkin's mind that the helpful spirit of Gilmor Brown lives on at the Pasadena Playhouse.

Betty Jean Morris shares that same view. As house manager of the playhouse, Betty Jean has had plenty of opportunity to witness Gilmor's antics. She stressed, "Gilmor is a good ghost. It's a shame, but anything untoward that happens at the theater is almost always blamed on Gilmor. He never does any harm, but he does play tricks."

With something of a protective tone, Betty Jean went on to explain that she has always felt extremely safe in the theater—even when she has had to be there late at night. For this reason, she's come to assume that the spirit of Gilmor likes her and appreciates her efforts. "I try very hard to please Gilmor; after all, he still looks after his theater."

Betty Jean has kept a record of some of the phantom's tricks—including the time that she "was trying to open the main door to the theater with my key. It would not unlock, [even] after many tries." Annoyed and puzzled, the woman simply "went away for a few minutes and, upon returning, tried again and it opened right away."

The majority of Gilmor's pranks simply seem to be attention-getters. There was the night, for instance, when Betty Jean was alone in the theater and her binoculars disappeared from the counter where she'd placed them only moments before.

Gilmor's presence is acknowledged by virtually everyone who works at the theater. A member of the box office staff was feeling frustrated because no matter how hard she tried she could not get her night's accounting to balance. Finally, in exasperation, she said aloud, "Not now, Gilmor." The columns of figures balanced on her next attempt.

Another box office employee, Doug Senior, credits Gilmor with finding a document that had been missing for months. Senior recounts that on and off for many weeks he had been searching for a particular piece of paper. One day, a shelf near where he was sitting fell. As he was tidying up the mess that resulted, he found the papers that had previously eluded his search.

An assistant to theater architect Dick McCann once set a file out on a table. He intended to discuss its contents with his boss, but before doing so went to the men's room. When he came out, moments later, the file had been moved to the banister of the stairs in the lobby. As no one else had been near the lobby area, it is now generally accepted that Gilmor put the file there—perhaps to remind the man of his original mission.

Gilmor doesn't just help others with their work. It's thought that he also still goes to his former office on the third floor of the building. Someone, or something, has to be in the apparently empty elevator that frequently, and mysteriously, travels up to that level.

Further proof of Betty Jean Morris' assessment about Gilmor's spirit still being actively involved in running the theater has been witnessed on numerous occasions. Projection booth employees were most annoyed during one production when their equipment was being tampered with during intermissions. Betty Jean remembered, "They locked the door [to the projection booth] when they left for intermission and the items were rearranged. They decided to post an usher next to the locked door during intermission to see who might be doing it. No one entered the booth and [yet] the items were still rearranged."

The house manager continued, "During a particular show, and always on a Sunday matinee, at exactly the same time for about three weeks, the house lights came on during the show. The master electrician examined everything and no one ever figured out why the house lights were coming on."

In the September 2000 edition of *FATE* magazine, actor/director Richard Vath recalled an incident in which he was preparing for a scene in the play *Dracula*. After rehearsing the segment in a particular manner, a banging sound, loud enough to stop the rehearsal, was heard reverberating throughout the auditorium. Vath immediately realized what was happening and said, out loud, "Okay, Gilmor, it's wrong. Let me do it another way."

As good as his word, Richard Vath changed the scene, and all was quiet. He did have one regret, though: "it occurred to me that the least I could have done was to give Gilmor credit in the program for his help."

It's Gilmor's presence that's thought to be the source of the otherwise inexplicable cold spots that randomly materialize around the theater, as well as doors that slam closed when no one's near them and disembodied footsteps that mysteriously walk about in otherwise empty areas of the theater. People who have encountered the ghost even feel that they've also seen something but, perhaps reflecting Gilmor's current supernatural incarnation, are unable to describe exactly what it is they've seen.

It is clear to almost everyone involved with the Pasadena Playhouse today that in his *after*life, Gilmor Brown is just as involved with the theater as he was in his life.

Walker in the 'Round

The logic behind the name "Theater 'Round The Corner" is simple. The theater is located around the corner from the main square in downtown Huntsville, Alabama. The history of the century-old building that houses the theater is not quite as straightforward. Theater employees Pat Tatum and Molly Pettis explained that the building was originally constructed as a livery stable, then was converted to a retail sales outlet. It was a "big warehousey-kind of thing" that had sat empty for over 20 years prior to 1995 when renovations to create the theater began.

Molly acknowledged that she is convinced the place "is haunted from those earliest days. Sometimes it sounds like there's a horse in there."

The more prominent ghost is not a horse, but the spirit of a man. Molly explained that, in her position as a seamstress and production assistant with the Theater 'Round The Corner, she's intimately familiar with the place. "It's a large building, a 200-seat theater, and there's an equally large space in the back where we work and then there are several smaller rooms around that. I work in one of those and I'll go in there when there is nobody else in the building except me. I've never felt uncomfortable, but I have definitely heard [inexplicable] things."

Those mysterious sounds have actually driven Kevin Parker, the theater's technical manager, from the building. Molly set the stage, so to speak, for Kevin to tell of his encounter. "He said he was working one evening late with another member of the staff when he had to go to the back room to get something."

Kevin continued, "When I went to the back room I heard the ghost walking around [above me]. The hair on the back of my neck stood up and I had to leave. It scared me silly that time."

To give Kevin credit, he did not go too far from the theater. Molly, who at the time was just making her way to the theater, found him "standing out front, smoking a cigarette. He looked kind of a little worried and I asked him, 'What's going on?' "

The slightly distraught man explained that he'd been working in the auditorium when he realized that he needed some additional wood from a workroom backstage. The moment he entered the room he knew something was wrong, or different, in that area. Molly related that Kevin "felt a very strange presence" in the room. Moments later, he became the first theater employee to hear the ghostly footsteps walk across the attic floor directly above his head. These disembodied footfalls have become a recognizable and common occurrence at the haunted Theater 'Round The Corner.

Molly continued, "We all have been in the theater alone or with just a couple of people and heard somebody in the attic—when there's been no one else in the building. It's not like birds or animal sounds. It's clearly someone walking. I can usually recognize people's gait, and when I'm in the sewing room I can hear somebody walking on a concrete floor but with a totally different gait than those I know. I get the sense from the gait that it's a fairly tall, stout man, probably very healthy—definitely a man. I'll get up and look, and there'll be no one there, and I just think, *Oh well, it's just the ghost.*"

Molly is so sure that the noises are caused by a ghost that out of respect for its existence she actually acknowledges the phantom by speaking out loud to it. "Hey, howya doin'?" she'll ask the invisible presence. "Then I'll just go back to what I was doing," she explains.

To confirm that her feelings were accurate, Molly invited a psychic friend to tour the building with her. His reaction was quick and sure. "Oh, yes, it's clear that there's [paranormal] stuff going on here in this place," he stated emphatically.

Although everyone on staff agrees the spirit in the attic is that of a man, Molly explained that she "is the only one who has ever seen anything. I was working about midnight one night. I wasn't tired though," she added, perhaps to forestall any possible skepticism about the validity of her experience. "I walked out into the main part of the workroom and just saw this sort of, I don't want to say mist, just this kind of disturbance in the air. It was really strange. It made me feel a little uneasy but I'm pretty accepting of those things. After that, I did see it [the inexplicable disturbance in the air] a couple of times in different parts of the theater."

Not all the employees are as comfortable with the specter. Molly described an encounter with the ghost that left one man determined not to be alone in the building ever again. The man arrived at the theater early one Saturday to do some work in the wood shop, which Molly explained was "just off the rehearsal space and adjacent to the attic stairs and door. He had been busy sawing for about an hour when he turned the saw off and began gathering the pieces he needed. At that time, he heard someone walk down the attic steps and stop at the door. He says that he looked around the corner expecting the door to open. It didn't, so he went to the door and opened it. No one was there."

This anonymous, and now rather shaken, employee stated that he "walked up the stairs and looked around. The lights were off and no one was there. The hair on my neck rose. I felt very uncomfortable—almost sad. I closed the building and left. I won't work here by myself anymore."

Tina, an administrative worker at the theater, reports that she regularly hears footsteps above her office. Molly recalled, "She describes it as a man taking three steps, then opening a door." The kicker in this description, though, is that "there is no door over the office area." Not surprisingly, the woman is reluctant "to go upstairs or to other parts of the building besides the office, when working alone."

The phantom footsteps have also been heard over the lobby "at the front of the building where there is no walk space or doors."

Even one of the theater's owners—a confirmed skeptic—admits that he "cannot explain the fact that he was alone, locking up the building after an evening performance, when he heard the same 'step, step, step' and a door opening right above the theater entrance. He couldn't explain it, but he left very quickly."

Whether it is the influence of the ghost or just part of the magic of a theater, certain productions at the Theater

'Round The Corner seem more charged than do others. As an example, Molly Pettis acknowledged, "We've recently done shows like *Dracula* and *The Turn of the Screw*—both are very intense but there was this very unusual intensity about them."

The fact that this theater is so special is overwhelmingly viewed as a positive quality by the staff. "It's been an interesting experience, and we joke about it, but I've always thought it was pretty neat."

No one knows the identity of the man, or the horse, who continue to haunt the building, but with such an accepting and even welcoming atmosphere, the Theater 'Round The Corner and its ghosts should all live together happily ever after.

SCENE VI

Pumphouse Phantoms

General manager Leslie Holth explained that, while only one of the ghost stories from the Pumphouse Theatres in Calgary, Alberta, had ever been published, many others have been "passed from ear to ear over the past 30 years."

Considering the structure's history, it's not much of a surprise that it has collected its share of resident spirits. Built in 1913 as Pumphouse #2, the place was a maze of pipes that drew water from the adjacent Bow River to supply the needs of Calgarians. Rumor is that at least one worker died in the building during those early years. By the mid-1920s the city's primary water source shifted from the Bow to the Elbow River and old #2 station was no longer viable. Nevertheless, the building was not demolished.

With its long and varied history, it's no wonder this building is haunted.

Inevitably, the building deteriorated. When the Great Depression cut its swath across the land, the still solid structure, with its proximity to the railroad tracks, became an unofficial but adequate temporary accommodation for hoboes resting from riding the rails.

Although we'd all like to believe that everyone who suffered through the Depression was a paragon of virtue—merely a victim of circumstance down on his or her luck—such was not the case. Most vagrants did not have much in the way of possessions and some had even less respect for life. Their understanding of justice tended not to rely upon formal sources. As a result, many thefts, fights, fatal accidents and even murders often went unnoticed and certainly unreported. Most people who accept that the Pumphouse Theatre facility is haunted feel the ghosts hail from that era and those circumstances.

By the late 1960s, the building had outlived its official and unofficial usefulness and was scheduled to be torn down. By coincidence, about that time drama teacher and advocate Joyce Doolittle "discovered" the site. She led an enthusiastic group of workers through needed renovations, and in 1972 the venue staged its first live production. Since then, the operation has flourished and become a multi-stage facility, collectively known as the Pumphouse Theatres.

All this success has perhaps amused the theater's longstanding ethereal residents. In 1979, then-manager Bob Eberle stated, "We may have a new theater, but the ghosts of the past still haunt us."

That statement is apparently as true today as it was more than two decades ago. Leslie Holth explained that "during a performance…the director was sitting in the audience when the house lights went to black. In the seconds before the stage lights went up, music was heard over the loudspeakers. Normally this would not be a problem, but the director had specifically not included music when the play opened. During intermission, the director stormed into the control booth demanding to know who had decided to add last-minute music to her show. Both the sound operator and the stage manager were dumbfounded. They hadn't turned on any music and, in fact, were equally confused by the mysterious [musical] presence."

That incident, along with the following one, might indicate that at least one of the manifestations in the Pumphouse is (or was) a music lover. According to the theater's website, the "wife of one of the employees was in the Joyce Doolittle Theatre lobby and heard…what sounded like a music box playing in the corner. She called her husband and asked if any music was being played in the dressing room or the theater. He told her 'no' and inquired as to why [she would ask]."

The woman explained that she had clearly heard distinct musical sounds. The employee was stunned. His wife would have had no idea that the area where she heard the music had contained a player piano, until it was recently auctioned off. The enigma was never solved.

Leslie Holth adds that "over the years, several employees and theater volunteers have noted the occasional 'visitation.' Sudden cold; hairs rising on the back of your neck; sounds coming from the darkened theater; the sounds of footsteps and laughter have all been reported or experienced. Although many people dismiss the possibility, there are those of us who verbally greet the building's 'residents' upon opening the doors each morning. Who knows? I'd rather be safe than sorry."

In conclusion, Leslie explained her philosophy of respect and acceptance. "They say we should befriend that which we don't know and thereby will come to appreciate a greater understanding of our world." With human compassion like that overseeing their haunted area, it's not much wonder the ghosts choose to remain at the Pumphouse.

Rude Wraith

A skeptic could claim that the following ghostly legend has endured only because it cannot, by now, be disproved. While that skeptical view might be correct, the story of the ghost at the old Metropolitan Opera House in New York City is too entertaining not to be retold. Some of the details surrounding the phantom have been lost in the mists of time, but accounts of Madame Alda's extremely annoying habits have certainly been duly recorded.

In her lifetime, Frances Alda was a diva, with all the implications, both negative and positive, that the term implies. The soprano was renowned around the world for her voice and for her stage presence. Those involved with the productions in which Madame Alda sang were often subjected to her well-honed superior attitude and haughty sense of self-importance, characteristics that apparently followed her into the great beyond.

The best-documented visitation by Alda's ghost occurred early in the opera season in 1955. A woman whose companion was unexpectedly unable to accompany her turned the spare ticket in at the box office. By intermission that solo patron had become extremely irate and she sought out the head usher. It seemed that the person who bought the ticket for the seat next to her disregarded every rule of audience etiquette.

The angry woman described a ring-laden dowager who voiced disparaging comments every time the evening's female lead began to sing. Worse, she would punctuate her every comment with an elbow to the patron's ribs. Even when other performers took the stage, this incredibly rude person would fidget with her program, thereby causing a further disturbance.

Understandably, the woman, who was already disappointed not to be attending the opera with her friend, wanted the administration of the hall to do something about this intolerable distraction. Those in authority were willing to do so, but their actions were certainly not what the patron had expected they would be. Rather than warning the nuisance that her behavior would no longer be permitted, a director of the house took the complainant aside. After giving her a glass of sherry, the employee explained to the woman that she would be able to enjoy the rest of the opera in peace. He knew this fact because the perpetrator was well-known to the staff at the Met. She was the ghost of the long-deceased prima donna Frances Alda, who had never been known to stay past the first act.

The haunted old building was replaced in 1966 and that change seems to have freed the discourteous spirit to move on, hopefully to a happier place where she perhaps perpetually performs in a starring role.

Where Has Vaughn Gone?

When all else was dark and quiet, the distinctive sounds of high-heeled shoes would echo through the University Playhouse on the campus of the University of Missouri in Kansas City. Those involved with the theater were never frightened by the phantom footsteps because they knew it was only Vaughn, the theater's resident ghost, walking about.

Dr. Vincent Scasselliti, Professor Emeritus, was associated with the theater for years prior to his retirement, but he never experienced a ghostly encounter himself. He did know colleagues who had been acquainted with Vaughn in life and later maintained that they heard her spirit throughout the building.

True to his academic background, Dr. Scasselliti noted that this ghost story was a legend and that he had nothing more than word of mouth to back it up. Having set this disclaimer in place, he kindly related that many years ago, "the University Playhouse productions were cast by both students and by community people. Vaughn apparently was a member of the KC [Kansas City] community who was in a variety of plays at the university. She passed out at an audition and died of a heart attack. The legend goes that [in life] Vaughn always wore high-heeled shoes, and [a faculty member] who retired many years ago claims that, in the old playhouse, several times, very late at night, he would hear the click, clack, clack of high heels down the hallway."

The building was torn down in 1978, 21 years after Vaughn's death, but the ghost has not been forgotten. In the book *Dead Zones,* the costume designer for the theater company explained that he would not go near the catwalk when he was alone at night because that was where he most often saw Vaughn's ethereal form.

The ghost looked so real that those unfamiliar with the story would see her image and naively ask who the woman sitting at the top of the catwalk steps was. Such a curious rookie would always be informed that he or she had seen the theater's ghost.

Just before demolition proceedings began at the playhouse, a group of people interested in tracking down the ghost spent some time in the auditorium. During a séance they held, the stage manager felt that Vaughn's spirit tried to come out to the group through his body. That decidedly uncomfortable sensation quickly diminished the man's interest in ghost hunting and caused him to leave the group.

The people who had gathered that night also heard what they thought was the ticking of a clock. This sound was quite puzzling because they were all sure there was no clock anywhere nearby. It wasn't until after the meeting that they realized the sound they'd heard was actually Vaughn walking among them. The rhythmic clicking that they presumed was being made by a clock was in fact the distinctive sound of the long-deceased actress' shoes.

Also before the playhouse was to be torn down a television crew decided to capture, for posterity, some film footage of the theater that had meant so much to both the academic community and Kansas City's citizens. When they developed the film they shot that night, they were delighted to find that Vaughn's image had appeared for her final curtain call. Rolling the footage at slow motion revealed the image of a woman, wearing a white gown, posing at the top of the catwalk stairs.

Historian Dr. Bill Worley explained that all that remains of the old playhouse are the comedy and tragedy masks that once graced the theater. Now they adorn the wall of the building that is closest to where the haunted theater once stood. "People probably don't even notice them today," Dr. Worley commented.

True, living people might not, but perhaps to Vaughn the ghost they are sufficient homage to mark the place she once loved and once haunted.

SCENE IX

Bob's in the House

Broken Arrow, Oklahoma, southeast of Tulsa, is home to the Broken Arrow Community Players. Although the troupe moved from their haunted auditorium in 1995, both the eerie old place and its ghost are still fondly remembered by everyone involved with the place.

Playhouse office manager Linda Tabberer responded to an initial question about the haunting in their former "house" with a warm chuckle and the comment, "Oh, yes, whenever anyone heard anything weird, they would say it was the ghost." Given the quirkiness of the story, it is no wonder that the ghost and his story are still remembered.

Theater people are often multi-talented and involved with many different aspects of production. Although Bob

Plumb earned his living as a classroom teacher, he was one of those who knew and loved virtually every aspect of live theater. At the time of his death in 1979, Bob was actively involved in the workings of the Broken Arrow Community Playhouse.

On the night of Bob Plumb's death, several theater board members saw doors in the auditorium inexplicably fly open and then close. They reported feeling as though someone was watching them when, in fact, they were alone in a room. Occasionally, even years after, people continued to feel a presence in the theater when they could see no one. All were quite convinced that the ghost of Bob Plumb was the source of the eerie experiences.

Some folks were so bothered by these mysterious goings-on that they took Bob's portrait down from the wall of the theater office. A few days after the painting had been removed and put into storage, it was found, hung up again, exactly where it had been before. Nobody ever owned up to moving the painting, so no explanation was found for this strange occurrence.

In the spring of 1988, another jack-of-all-theater-trades named Bob was working late at night painting props. Suddenly Bob Riley felt as though he was not alone in the building. A glance into the seating area confirmed that his feeling was correct, for there, in a very recognizable form, sat Bob Plumb, or at least his ghostly image. The apparition was so lifelike that Riley nearly greeted the man before realizing that what he was gazing upon could not be the man he'd known. It could only be his specter. Bob Riley hastily packed up his painting supplies, left the theater and went straight home.

Perhaps the most dramatic proof of Bob Plumb's after-death involvement with the theater came in the form of an application from a volunteer. A young man came to the theater to ask if he might somehow volunteer his services around the place. He readily admitted that he had no theatrical background or experience. The applicant added that he had just recently moved and that, strangely, ever since his move, he had felt a strong desire to become involved with the theater group.

Tom Berenson, a local journalist who was active with the playhouse, looked at the details the potential volunteer had included on his information card. He could hardly believe his eyes. This young man, the one with no previous theater experience, the one whose interest in the theater had only surfaced after a recent move, gave his address as 119 South Jackson—the very house where Bob Plumb had lived and died.

It certainly appears that, for several years after his death, the spirit of Bob Plumb continued his involvement with the Broken Arrow Community Players—both from the theater and from his home.

"SALT" of the Afterlife

The legends are as old and as exquisite as the theater itself. The Syracuse Area Landmark Theater (SALT) was built in 1928. To say it is a splendid edifice would be to badly understate the truth. Referred to as both an "Indo-Persian-Hindu temple" and a "Shangri-La," the nearly 3000-seat theater was certainly something set a world apart from its location in downtown Syracuse, New York. To step into the foyer was to step into a magical time and place.

Sadly, through the passage of years this beautiful building fell upon hard times. By the early 1970s, the owners had already sold both the magnificent chandelier that once graced the lobby and the grand pipe organ that had provided music before, during and after theatrical presentations. Despite these efforts to pump money back into the business, Loew's State Theatre, as it was then known, was headed for financial disaster. By the mid-1970s, the theater building was slated for demolition (in classic Joni Mitchell lyric style, to put up a parking lot). This was a doubly dreadful shame because the building had also long been home to a ghost. The phantom's image was noted on a summer's night in 1978 after the audience had left the building and only four stagehands (Mark de Lawyer, Phil Spadaro, Jerry Haber and Mike Reynolds) remained behind. They were standing on the stage chatting when, from the periphery of his vision, Spadaro thought he spotted an image—an image of a young woman dressed in white, sitting in a balcony seat.

The man called up to the presence and advised her that the theater was closed and she should not still be there, that she should have left some time ago. As if in response, and without protest, the specter stood up and glided down the aisle to its center before disappearing from the men's vision. Rather badly unnerved, the men finished what they had to do and left the theater.

Although the badly dilapidated building was home to someone's spirit, all hope of saving the once-grand theater seemed lost until a group of concerned citizens banded together to preserve and restore the edifice. The group worked quickly and efficiently to have the theater protected from destruction by having it added to the National Register of Historic Places. But the work of these dedicated volunteers had only begun. The paperwork might have been successfully completed but now a tremendous amount of physical labor lay ahead.

Even in the earliest stages of the massive and much-needed renovations, the house ghost was noticed again. A member of the theater's board of directors called in a psychic named Barb Verna, who was not at all surprised to hear that people had begun to recognize that supernatural spirits were in the place. Barb felt that a female specter in the balcony was the strongest supernatural presence. The psychic immediately identified this manifestation as a woman who had been married to a theater employee. The woman longed for a career on the stage, but she only obtained bit roles in the theater. She loved the entertainment hall so much in life that she had no desire to leave the building after her death.

Feeling she had explained that enigma as best she could, Verna went on to describe an anomaly in the physical structure of the building. She spoke of a rather garish room with walls originally adorned with small pieces of colored glass that had, since the time of its first incarnation, been painted entirely red. Unknown to this psychic was that such a room had just been uncovered, although no one knew why or when its doorway had been sealed over.

From the psychic landscape of the area around that hidden room, Verna was able to inform the board member that there had been at one time a bouquet of flowers on a shelf in the room and a rather large mirror on a wall. The woman who used the area had a habit of combing her hair while gazing into that mirror.

As the sensitive Verna probed her psychic awareness more and more, she was able to reveal that the ghost from that boarded-up room traveled all over the building and especially liked to attend (and subtly influence) meetings held by the new board of directors.

The theater's subterranean cellar was an eerie area, even without a ghost. The basement was an unlit series of cave-like tunnels that were flooded in places. Although spooky in its own right, the basement also had paranormal activity. Disembodied voices often accompanied unexplainable gusts of chilly air.

Lynne May, another area woman gifted with psychic abilities, determined that many supernatural vibrations were in the building and that all were good, with the exception of two areas: the "Walnut Room," which had once been a lounge, and the recently discovered "Red Room." She sensed that at some time in the history of the latter room, blood had been spilled.

Less clairvoyantly gifted employees noted that a flashlight would mysteriously stop working when the person carrying it walked past one of those two rooms. Inexplicable balls of light and, more commonly, the transparent image of a woman have been observed near both rooms.

Today, management and staff at the Syracuse Area Landmark Theater prefer their paranormal presences to have a lower profile than before. Fortunately for lovers of ghostly theater lore (and, of course, for the ghosts themselves), the legendary stories have been well-preserved.

STILL APPEARING

Phantom at the Bagdad

The Bagdad Theater has been a landmark in Portland, Oregon, for nearly three-quarters of a century. Built in 1927, the theater incorporated the "Arabian Nights" design that was so popular at the time. Actors including the dashing Douglas Fairbanks starred in blockbuster silent movies such as his classic *Thief of Bagdad*. No doubt there were those in the mid-1920s who considered the expenditure of $100,000 in construction costs for a public auditorium as highly exorbitant, but overall the community's reaction was welcoming. A local scribe of the day declared the lush building to be "a triumph of artistry and craftsmanship."

Exactly when the Bagdad Theater first became haunted is difficult to pin down. Legend has it that many years ago a theater custodian hanged himself from one of the exposed rafters in the building. This gruesome tale is sufficient reason for the huge theater to be haunted. Furthermore, the scuttlebutt goes on to explain that, for years after the tragic event, the very rope the suicide victim used to kill himself remained hanging from the beam where his lifeless body had once dangled. This background, in addition to reports of eerie events over the years, leaves little question that the Bagdad is home to spirits.

Tim Hills, historian for the theater, acknowledged that "the staff is pretty sure some otherworldly force is in residence." Support for that belief lies in numerous reports of

An otherworldly presence is thought to inhabit this theater.

strange goings-on in the building, many of which have become recognizable as indications of a ghostly presence. For instance, shortly after the theater was rewired, the master switch was turned off, effectively shutting down all electricity flowing into the building. As expected, the lights immediately began to go dark. Seconds later, the same lights came back on and, for roughly an hour, all the lighting fixtures in the Bagdad flickered on and off. Eventually all the lights went dark, but no earthly explanation was ever found for this oddity. Electrical anomalies are a common occurrence when a ghost is present, but the oddity wasn't really too surprising in a place reputed to be haunted.

A staff washroom on the second floor is traditionally a particularly unpopular place with employees because it has no ventilation into or from it. Despite this absence of air flow, inexplicable drafts, actually described once as "a cold wind," have been known to rush through this self-contained room. The force of these mysterious air currents has been strong enough, according to witnesses, that both toilet paper and cotton towels on a roll flap in the breeze.

Whether the ghost is that of the former caretaker or not, his or her presence is certainly welcome to stay. Not only is the entity accepted by staff members but, with a seating capacity of 700, the place is certainly large enough to remain uncrowded and haunted at the same time.

SCENE II

It's a Wonderful (After)life

Chicago's Music Box Theatre first opened for business in August 1929, just a few weeks before the stock market crashed, heralding the start of the Great Depression. The downtown theater's size may have been an important factor in its survival. At 800 seats, compared to many 3000-seat theaters of the era, the movie palace was almost intimate. This size might have contributed to sufficient box office receipts that kept the auditorium functioning for more than 50 years.

Over the years a great deal has been written about the theater's elaborate architectural styling. A current representative of the Music Box described the interior most succinctly by suggesting that it was intended to visually transport members of the audience, via a depiction of perfect weather conditions, to an idyllic outdoor courtyard. Could there be a better place to spend one's eternity? Whitey thinks not.

Longtime theater associate Chris Carlo explained the resident presence this way: "There's not much spooky to tell about Whitey. He's a very caring spirit."

For more than 50 years, Whitey, the resident wraith, was the theater's manager. He left his mark on the business in a very positive and enduring way. "There are a couple of adults still in the neighborhood who actually worked for him," Chris explained. Sadly, the loyal manager died in the theater on the eve of Thanksgiving Day, 1977.

Given his history, it's really no wonder that his lingering spirit is very protective of the place. Whitey's specter has been credited with helping the staff in various ways. His presence is felt especially strongly along aisle four by the side doors where, over the years, generations of children tried to sneak in to see a movie.

Whitey's amenable ghostly nature can occasionally be pushed too far. Carlo explained that the phantom "expresses his displeasure at a bad theater organist" by suddenly lowering the curtains around both organ chambers at once. Beyond that one sensitive issue, the spirit can be generally counted on to be of assistance.

"My partner and I have been friends of Whitey's for 18 years now," Chris continued. "We invoke his help when things go wrong in the old building. He always points the way to the problem, if not its solution."

In thanks for all his dedication to the theater, both before and after his death, Whitey has been granted the title Manager Emeritus. What more could a soul ask for than to spend his entire afterlife in a beautiful building that he knew and loved, where both his memory and his presence are revered?

Lyrical Ghosts

If you travel north approximately 90 kilometers (just more than 60 miles) from London, England, you'll come to Wellingborough, Northamptonshire, home to the haunted Lyric Theatre. There is no question whether or not this auditorium has a ghost. The only unknown pertains to who the spirit is.

The Lyric was built in 1936, but the haunting may date back to the 1800s when the Cheese Lane Congregational Chapel and its affiliated cemetery occupied the land. In 1903, the bodies and accompanying headstones from the graveyard were carefully relocated and the church building was converted to a cheese production plant. One of those whose final resting place was disturbed may have been upset enough about the upheaval that its spirit has stayed behind.

Although only a single story remains to support that theory, it is certainly one that deserves some thought. Anne Lockwood of Wellingborough and Ron Smith of Kettering were raised near the cheese factory. In typical childhood form, despite severe warnings from their parents, they and other neighborhood children would wait at a particular spot where they were hidden from view but could clearly see the area that is now the back of the Lyric. When they waited patiently, their efforts were rewarded with a retrocognitive experience. Not only did the ghost appear, but the whole scene before their eyes shifted to a time long before any of them were born.

They saw a solitary soldier wearing a uniform. They all knew they were seeing not a living person but an enigma from a previous time period. His image was hazy and he was silently walking along a cobblestone street that no longer existed. After each brief sighting, the image vanished suddenly.

According to the book *Phantoms of the Theater* (by Robert Lamott-Brown), a more modern and considerably better documented theory suggests that the entity at the Lyric might be the soul of a former factory or theater manager—a man who had hanged himself at work. Although his name and the date of his death are not easily accessible now, reports of the ghost sightings certainly are.

Sheila LeFevre, a concession worker at the theater, told a reporter for a local newspaper that she had seen the ghost "several times" during her tenure at the Lyric.

Other articles ran in the more widely circulated *Evening Telegram* on various dates in October 1969. Maintenance worker Mick Lamb came close to quitting the job he otherwise enjoyed when he came too near the ghost. Lamb described standing in awe and terror as he watched a "hazy...human form" sitting on a narrow perch, high above the stage. The image was clear enough that the worker was able to make out the ghost's brown jacket and lighter-colored trousers.

When seven people held a vigil in the theater, one of them, Violet West, explained that they had seen an inexplicable image on the balcony. Everyone in the group knew that what they'd seen couldn't have been human because "it was like a white shadow" that darted "from one side of the foyer balcony to another" before disappearing from view.

This is the same place in the theater where manager Barbara Mansfield observed the apparition. Initially Mansfield "felt a presence." This strange sensation caused her to stop what she'd been doing and look around her. "Something [was] going across the balcony." The woman called out, asking the form to identify itself, but received no reply. Fearing she might have been the brunt of a practical joke, Mansfield simply dismissed the incident until her next sighting of the image. That was when Barbara Mansfield lost her skepticism and came to believe that her place of employment was home to a ghost.

Likely in response to the frequent articles in the *Evening Telegram,* a spokesperson for the West Hertfordshire Psychical Research Group published the following rather heated statement: "the scoffing has got to stop. A ghost really does haunt [the Lyric]." People from the Research Group equipped with cameras, audio recorders and thermometers had spent a night in the place. During that time, they experienced a sighting and, during a Ouija board session, direct communication as the phantom reached out from his plane to ours.

The group was distressed to read the first word the ghost spelled out: "help." Only moments later, the name "Daniel" was added to the message. At the same time, two red lights were seen moving slowly across the balcony. The orbs drew closer and closer together as they traveled on their separate trajectories before merging into a single glow.

On November 13, 1969 (which did not fall on a Friday), the newspaper published an article indicating that the restless spirit had made his wishes more clearly known when he asked, via a Ouija board, to have his remains blessed by a priest.

All this certainly supports those who are sure the place is haunted, but it really doesn't clarify whose spirit is left behind. Anne Lockwood and Ron Smith, who related seeing the ghost nearly 20 years before the theater was built, had one last piece of information that might be the missing piece of the puzzle. The siblings recalled that a family, including two sons, lived in a nearby residence. One of those brothers was killed during World War 1. As he lay dying, he allegedly proclaimed that he would return to his home. His name was Daniel.

• • •

The venue in Northamptonshire is not the only haunted theater named "Lyric." When I phoned the Lyric Theater in Blacksburg, Virginia, executive director Susan Mattingly acknowledged that although she remains skeptical, legend has it that their building is haunted. Examination of different reports over the years would certainly support that theory. The theater, a portion of a much larger and very impressive-looking building, opened its doors on April 17, 1930. By the time the place closed as an entertainment venue in the 1980s, the auditorium was in serious disrepair. It was also very haunted.

A man named Joel (sometimes referred to as Jay) Furr had personal knowledge of the theater as it existed just before it closed. Based on his own information and experiences at that time, Furr has written extensively about the building and its ghosts. Virtually all of what Furr reported from his experiences has recurred on more recent occasions.

One night in the late 1980s, just after the last movie had finished running, the couple who ran the theater at that time (Bud and Beth) were going through their usual closing routine before locking the theater down for the night. While Beth was otherwise occupied, Bud heard what he presumed was the end of a conversation between two patrons. As a courtesy, he waited out of sight until the two voices ceased talking. Moments later, he expected to see these people coming down the stairs. When he didn't, the man checked the area and found it to be as empty as he had initially presumed it should be. No one has ever been able to explain this strange incident.

During that same era, clusters of people, each of whom knew that they were alone in a locked building, have reported hearing loud screams coming from a balcony area near the projection booth. These folks have actually taken comfort from their assumption that the source responsible for the cries is nothing more dangerous than a woman's ghost. Occasionally the horrible sounds will be accompanied by something even more unnerving—a woman's voice pleading "let me out, let me out."

Although she may not realize it, that horribly distraught soul is not alone beyond the curtain of time in the theater. Enigmatic sounds of heavy footsteps have been heard both in the balcony area and in a back stairwell that once connected the balcony to the projection booth. These sounds reverberate throughout the theater even when it is known to be empty except for those frightened listeners. Perhaps an even more disturbing sensation is when a cold draft brushes past people who happen to be on the stairs. This phenomenon is often followed by the sight of sourceless shadows and the sound of almost imperceptible "mutterings."

Possibly to explain away these sounds, a legend evolved around them. A story about a worker who fell to his death during construction of the building became generally accepted. It was and is presumed that his soul has never left the theater. Although that is almost as common a "reason" for a haunting as the old classic about a building being erected upon a native burial site, not everyone accepted the legend as true. Detractors continued to doubt the story until a woman came in expressing interest in any old photos the theater had. It seems that her grandfather was a construction worker on the site who was killed as the result of a fall.

Another person associated with the Blacksburg Lyric who has experienced inexplicable events is Robert Sebek, a member of the restored theater's board of directors. Sebek heard "many weird noises" before and during the restoration in 1999, which saved the old showplace. Often those sounds seemed to come from the second floor where the administrative offices were initially housed. Although others disagree with him, Sebek feels that all the phantoms fled during the renovation process.

General manager Charles Morgan tends to disagree with Sebek's assessment, maintaining that there are as many strange goings-on in the theater now as there ever were. Morgan even goes so far as to specify the balcony as a particularly ghost-ridden area. He also maintains that one can still hear voices coming from storage rooms that were once parts of the old balcony.

The most recent ghostly exploration of the Lyric took place on June 25, 2001, when three people associated with a Blacksburg newspaper, the *Collegiate Times*, spent the night in the haunted theater. Reporter Scott Samson was accompanied by Shannon Dwyer as well as the newspaper's photo editor.

Their adventure began with a tour of the premises, and their guide was none other than general manager Charles Morgan. Samson, who approached this unusual assignment with light-hearted feelings, underwent quite an attitude readjustment as they moved about the darkened "house." In the upper balcony, Samson maintained a detached interest in what he was seeing and the words he was listening to from a man who knew the area intimately and had heard ghostly cries for help. Still, Samson remained unconvinced—until the trio and their guide approached the back stairwell that had so often been identified as being haunted. Something about that area, Samson later reported in the article he wrote, set his previously well-hidden ghost-hunting spirit into overdrive.

The tour ended just before midnight. As Monday, June 25 became Tuesday, June 26, Scott Samson and Shannon Dwyer entered the back stairway together. Their intrusion was greeted with a noisy growling sound that had Shannon fleeing for safety. Unfortunately, her flight was cut short: the only way to leave the area was by that same staircase. With the aid of Scott's coaxing, the two young people made their way down the stairs, all the while *very* aware that an unseen presence was with them in that enclosed area.

Scott felt pressure all around him. Then both he and Shannon heard footfalls. Someone was coming up the stairs toward them—although neither of them could see anyone. The sounds from an invisible but heavy individual came at them faster and faster. The once-brave pair was momentarily paralyzed with fear before they were able to flee from a supernatural force that clearly did not welcome them. The newspaper's photo editor was right behind them all the way out of the building.

Once the trio had calmed down, they were determined to re-enter the haunted building. As Samson so colorfully worded it in his article for the *Collegiate Times*, they "approached the door that separated mankind from the underworld." The frightened little group was no more than inches inside the building when the doors at the bottom of the stairs slammed shut, as did the door they'd just opened.

The group sat huddled together in the darkened theater, surrounded by emptiness and silence. It was 3 AM, one hour before their scheduled departure. That was when they heard an unseen door open and close. Those very distinctive noises were immediately followed by the sounds of someone entering the place. Sure that at least one friend of theirs was trying to play a practical joke on them, the adventurers prepared themselves for a confrontation. When none was forthcoming, they shined the beam from their flashlight all around the theater. The place was as empty (except for the three of them) as it had been when silence had prevailed.

After another moment or so was spent calming down, Scott asked whatever was out there to identify itself. Again, the door at the bottom of the stairs slammed closed. That seemed to be the phantom's concluding statement, for no further indications of ghostly presence were heard or felt that night.

Both Shannon and Scott came away from their overnight stay with changed attitudes. (The mindset of the photographer was not recorded.) Both people entered the building with skepticism and cynicism. They left the theater the following morning knowing that they had been in the presence of the ghosts at the Lyric Theatre in Blacksburg, Virginia. Perhaps now they'd enjoy a trip to Northamptonshire, England!

Walnut Street Wraith

Richard Vath is a multi-talented man. He is an award-winning writer who has also produced, directed and acted at a professional level. Perhaps one of the most interesting experiences in Vath's life revolved around a simple conversation he had with another actor.

Vath's colleague referred to a rumor he had heard about a highly skeptical young actor who ventured forth to stay overnight in a haunted theater. The skeptic no doubt wanted to prove his point that the east-coast theater was not haunted and that it could not be haunted because there was no such thing as ghosts. Unfortunately the daring actor was never able to publicly validate his claim. His lifeless body was discovered the following morning. The whole story behind the man's untimely death has never been sorted out, and it probably never can be. All that is known for certain is that his body was found in the orchestra pit, and he was dead from a broken neck.

The authorities were called in immediately, of course, but all that could be determined was that he had been drinking just prior to his death. It might be reasonable to

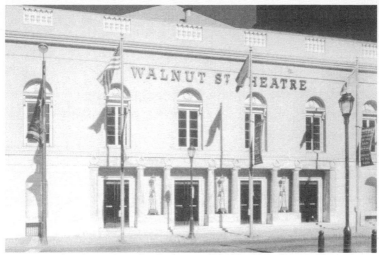
This theater is said to be haunted by the ghost of an actor.

assume that, in a presumably "tipsy" state, he fell from the stage. What was strange was that his injuries were "the same kind of fractures that hanging produces." That piece of information was all Richard Vath needed to conclude that the legendary theater being alluded to was the beautiful old Walnut Street Theatre in downtown Philadelphia.

Richard Vath was definitely in a position to make such a judgment, for he had actually *seen* a ghost in the Walnut Street venue. The theater was built in 1809 and, amazingly, has been in continuous operation since then.

When Vath played there "for an extended run," he became friendly with the doorman who, one evening, told him about the longstanding ghost story connected with the theater. It seemed that, just a few years after it was built, the auditorium became haunted by the spirit of an actor—the victim of unrequited love for an actress. Unable to bear the pain of his broken heart, the man fashioned a noose around one of the many supports high above the stage. After adjusting the knots and securing the rope around his neck, he stepped off the beam and into his life after death. Legend has it that his spirit has never left the theater.

After hearing the tale, Vath was intrigued enough to stay behind, long after closing time. He wanted to at least see, if not meet, the ghost. By 3 AM, Richard Vath's patience was rewarded when he watched a glow appear near stage left, close to the box seats. The inexplicable green-colored light moved slowly, and seemingly with purpose, up to the balcony area. Once there, the eerie glow transformed from a mere spot of light into the form of a man.

The image was clear enough that Vath was later able to report that the phantom was dressed in very old-fashioned clothing and acted in a way that revealed great sorrow. In a somewhat ironic twist, Vath surmised that the ghost was startled to realize he was not as alone in the building as he had expected he would be at that haunting hour. Vath's corporeal presence apparently caused the ethereal presence to "run"—or at least to disappear from the sight of mortal eyes.

Later, when discussing the sighting, Vath and the doorman who had tipped him off about the entity agreed that they both felt great sympathy for the spirit who seemed to have found no comfort in death, no escape from the pain he felt in life.

For the most part, those currently involved with the Walnut Street Theatre do not seem to be troubled by the ghost's presence. Perhaps, like many involved with the performing arts, these people feel that a theater can expect to have a ghost or even needs a ghost to be "legitimate."

We Three Ghosts

In 1892, southern evangelist Sam P. Jones, along with the recently converted riverboat captain Tom Ryman, completed construction of the mammoth Union Gospel Tabernacle in Nashville, Tennessee.

In 1904, when Captain Ryman died, the building was renamed in his honor. Given the intensity with which he lived—prior to Jones helping him find religion, the captain was a hard-drinking, hard-living gambler—it's not much of a surprise that, since his death, Tom's ghost has remained in the building that bears his name.

The long-deceased Captain Ryman's image has made itself visible on occasion and his spirit has also been heard calling out, presumably in displeasure, after stage performances that his converted soul could have construed as morally offensive. Perhaps this activity proves that, if there's anything more evangelical than a convert, it can only be the ghost of one!

Even without its namesake's continuing presence, the Ryman Auditorium deserves to be well haunted. Almost from its earliest years, renowned musicians, singers, dancers, actors and influential speakers displayed their talents on the Ryman stage. The opera *Carmen* was performed there in 1901. Six years later, President Teddy Roosevelt addressed those gathered at the Ryman. In 1914, Anna Pavlova danced her way into the hearts of an audience at the former revival hall. Toward the end of World War I, Charlie Chaplin, Mary Pickford and Douglas

Fairbanks promoted the purchase of Victory Bonds to help support the United States' war effort. Talents as diverse as Rudolph Valentino, Will Rogers, Ethel Barrymore, Nelson Eddy and Katharine Hepburn were only a few of the performers who delighted audiences at the Ryman before 1943 when the building became home to the Grand Old Opry.

From then until 1974, when the Opry moved to Opryland, country and western music lovers from all over the world flocked to Nashville to hear and see the very best in the field. This dramatic history has created an abundance of ghosts.

Brent Hyams, currently senior marketing manager at the Ryman, acknowledges that a commonly accepted legend claims Tom Ryman's spirit is only one of three entities haunting the auditorium. Although he has never had any firsthand experience himself, Hyams has heard and read several reports about these ghosts.

"There are lots of mysterious things that have happened around here," he explained. "Security officers who work here say that after one o'clock they start hearing things—footsteps. They go and check, but no one's there. None of the guards has ever been scared, really, except the woman who swears she saw Hank Williams Senior. Now whenever she goes through the area where she saw his image, she calls out, 'I'm coming through, don't scare me.' "

According to the July/August 2001 edition of a trade publication called *Live Sound*, a crew preparing for a production at the Ryman sensed that "there was a strange and inspirational feeling" in the theater's balcony. This area, known as the Confederate Gallery, was constructed in 1897 to honor the efforts of Confederate soldiers during the Civil War. Although members of the work crew did not know it at the time, the special aura they sensed was probably caused by the ghost of a Confederate soldier who is frequently seen in the balcony area.

Despite this odd "feeling," the workers continued to ready the place for the coming performance. As part of the overall rehearsal and sound check, Emmylou Harris sang one of the many ballads made famous by the Grand Old Opry star Hank Williams Senior. According to one witness, her rendition was "breathtaking." According to many others, it was followed by the sound of a single soul applauding. Despite a diligent search for the source of this applause, no one could find its origin.

When the house engineer at the Ryman told the group that the place was haunted, they were actually relieved and the ghost of Hank Williams Senior probably enjoyed the recognition he'd received. Emmylou Harris paid a heartfelt and beautiful tribute to the music that was the man's life, and the scrambled search for his presence indirectly acknowledged the existence of Hank Williams Senior, both in the afterlife and in the "house."

As of 2001, all the ethereal beings at the Ryman have effectively been granted considerable residential security, for the building was declared a National Historic Landmark. As the performances, both ethereal and corporeal, have been going on for more than a century, it seems safe to presume that the ghosts at the Ryman Auditorium will haunt it for the rest of their afterlives.

Wraith of the Great White Way

Lost souls, from both sides of the veil of time, wander New York City's theater district, particularly the ghostly Great White Way of Broadway. Some are ghosts of unfulfilled dreams; others are supernatural ghosts of unfulfilled dreamers. Many of these ghosts haunt the area's ornate theaters. The following ghost story spans the American countryside—and beyond to Europe where many of our entertainment traditions began. This ghost story is almost as detailed as the architecture of Broadway's magnificent New Amsterdam Theatre itself. But to view it with the most effective hindsight, we must begin the tale in Toronto, Canada, in the late 1800s.

• • •

Gladys Smith was an exceptionally beautiful little baby, but was born (on April 9, 1893) into poverty. Over the next five years, another daughter and then a son were born into the same Smith household. The limited resources available had to be spread even more thinly. Shortly after the boy, John, was born, Gladys' father, the family's breadwinner, was killed in an industrial accident.

Charlotte, the children's mother, was unable to earn enough money for the family on her own. That was hardly surprising, given the times. What *was* surprising was who stepped in to fill that role: the family's first-born. Although she was barely of school age at the time, Gladys began what was to become a monumentally successful and enduring career in acting. It wasn't long before the tiny, talented and determined entrepreneur's name was changed to the one we are now familiar with—Mary Pickford.

Mary's popularity among audiences gave her a position of power in her dealings with theater companies. It was soon obvious that the child's acting talents were overshadowed only by her abilities to master the entertainment industry's intricate business and financial aspects. As a result, directors were often faced with the tasks of adding roles and salaries for Mary's brother, sister and mother, all of whom had also changed their names from Smith to Pickford. Unfortunately, the rest of her family was not nearly as talented as Mary. Even more unfortunately, they *all* loved to overindulge in alcohol.

In addition to that liquid obsession, Jack Pickford, Mary's brother, also loved women, and one of the women he most loved (and eventually married) was Olive Thomas. She was a beautiful young dancer with Ziegfeld's Follies, the internationally acclaimed dance troupe that performed in Broadway's elegant New Amsterdam Theatre. "Flo" Ziegfeld demanded a great deal from his dancers and, like Jack Pickford, Ziegfeld loved women, most particularly Olive Thomas. Ziegfeld and Thomas had, according to Jackie Green of the New Amsterdam Theatre's staff, "a torrid affair."

Not long thereafter, Olive met Jack. She left the troupe *and* Ziegfeld to marry the wealthy, handsome, fun-loving young Pickford. The marriage did not work out well. In 1920, while on a Parisian holiday, a liquor-drenched evening turned fatal when Olive ingested poison. It is impossible now to piece together complete details of the tragedy.

Important facts were said to have been covered up at the time. Many of the details released to the public were contradictory. The gossip surrounding the incident was circuitous, possibly unfounded, but definitely gruesome.

Jack returned to America brokenhearted. That same year, Mary, the family's financial keeper, married Douglas Fairbanks. The couple resided in a Beverly Hills mansion, which they named Pickfair. Interestingly, this palatial home, which had once been a hunting lodge, was already haunted when they purchased it. Those ghosts were seen periodically over the years that Doug and Mary lived and lavishly entertained there. Since their deaths, both Mary and Doug's specters were seen in their beloved residence right up until the time it was demolished.

As Mary's career blossomed, Jack Pickford kept up his alcohol-fueled womanizing. He eventually married another member of the Ziegfeld Follies. Legend has it that the ghost of Olive Thomas came back to haunt the New Amsterdam Theatre. Maybe she wanted to keep an eye on Jack and his new wife. Or perhaps the dancer's soul just relished being back amidst the theatrical splendor of New York City's "crown jewel" of theaters.

Some say the beautiful phantom is still there in the Broadway hall that was so painstakingly and magnificently renovated in the mid-1990s. As a matter of fact, theater representative Jackie Green advises that "several staff have seen her," and that the story about the ghost of Olive Thomas is "covered in the [regular] theater tours."

The Victoria's Miss Vicky

As house manager of the elegant Victoria Theatre in Dayton, Ohio, David Hastings has worked with Miss Vicky for nearly three decades. He initially approached his new job in a haunted theater with a large dose of skepticism. David explained that, when he first took over his responsibilities at the Victoria, he simply "didn't believe in ghosts."

Those who'd been associated with the theater longer tried to prepare him for the new and probably inexplicable experiences he was no doubt about to have.

David recalls colleagues telling him that there was definitely a ghostly presence in the theater. " 'Oh, the place is haunted,' they'd say. 'You'll hear footsteps and you'll hear this and that and this will happen and so forth.' Of course I didn't believe any of it. I knew it was all hogwash."

David Hastings continued to be skeptical until something occurred that started him wondering. As he explained, "One evening, when I had been working, it wasn't late, it was around 10 o'clock, and I was leaving the theater. As I was coming down the main staircase, all the house lights were out and I heard footsteps on the stage. I thought that it was our technical director leaving at the same time as I was, so I called out to him 'good night.' There wasn't any answer and the steps continued. They didn't slow down or speed up…it was a dark house, and the only way to turn lights on was to go down to the stage…[but] my mother did *not* raise a fool—I was not going to go there."

David left the theater as quickly as he possibly could. He later asked the technical director if he had been walking across the stage at that time. The answer was an emphatic "no." The other man had been nowhere near the stage when David had heard the footfalls, but he did have a pretty strong conviction about the source of the sounds David had heard.

"John Renzel was our technical director at the time and he told me, 'Oh that was the ghost.' I said, 'Oh, bullwinkle.' He said, 'No, it was!' "

David terminated the conversation by telling Renzel flat out, "I don't believe it."

Despite his firmly skeptical stance, the spirit was already making headway into the new house manager's head and heart. "It was shortly after that instance that she started really making her presence known to me."

The ghost everyone now refers to as Miss Vicky is widely recognized as the spirit of an actress who, in the late 1800s or early 1900s, disappeared during the performance of a play in which she had a role. Between scenes, the woman hurried upstairs from the stage upstairs to her dressing room for a regular costume change. A security guard later reported having seen her, coming back down the stairs wearing the taffeta gown required for her next scene. She stopped in mid-staircase and told him, "I've forgotten my fan." The actress ran back upstairs for her prop and has never been seen since. It is presumed that she did manage to pick up her fan because both it and the taffeta dress she'd been wearing were also missing.

As there were only two ways to leave the theater from the woman's dressing room—either out a third-floor window or past the observant security guard—no one had any idea what happened to the actress.

David added that there was "no rhyme or reason as to why or how the disappearance happened. The Dayton newspapers have articles in their archives about the disappearance.

"She has never been seen, but you can hear the rustling of her gown as she moves through the theater. Sometimes she'll brush by your shoulder when you're going up or down a staircase. And then there's her perfume. You can be standing around talking with someone and there'll just be a faint fragrance wafting by, but there's no one [visible] there. This has not only happened to me; it's happened to a lot of the employees here and even a lot of the patrons here have experienced her. We're real happy that she's here. We had a renovation in 1988–90 and we were afraid that we were going to lose this energy, but she stuck around. As a matter of fact, she played a lot of pranks and tricks on the construction people while they were working."

Just before the two-year renovation closure began, Miss Vicky was in almost constant communication with one particular employee.

"When we were shutting down in June 1988, Kelly Franz, who was our marketing director at the time, was putting a slide show together for our final performance here before the theater shut down." The slide show included pictures "of old actors that had been here, and pictures of the theater, and what it had gone through, and so forth. Each night [after work], Kelly would lock her door. She'd have the slides on a light table. The next day, she would come in and the slides would be moved around. Kelly would move them back into the sequence that she'd had them in [the night before] and they would be moved around [again] the next day. This went on about four or five different times until, finally, Kelly left the slides in the order they'd been moved around to. They were never changed again."

Fortunately, David explained, the marketing director's reactions to this situation were entirely positive. "Kelly had quite a working, loving relationship with the energy. It [the spirit] has had more fun with Kelly than…with anyone [else]."

The next anecdote proved David's point very strongly. "While [the slides incident] was going on, Kelly's desk and chair would vibrate. Nothing else in her office or anywhere around would do it. One day during this time period, I was in my office and Kelly called me and she said, 'David you have to come up here right now,' so I go running up and she says 'sit down.' I sat down and I could feel the chair vibrate and her desk vibrate."

The presence continued her involvement with the slides right up to the actual show. "When we were doing our slide presentation, we had two slide projectors going. They would alternate back and forth, but for no reason at all the one projector stopped working completely. It had power and a bulb and everything, so we just had to switch the carousel to the other projector. We have no idea what could've caused that and so we just blamed the ghost. She didn't like what was going on."

Although she's never been seen, Miss Vicky did allow her presence to be captured by a film crew.

David recalled, "Three or four years ago, WDTN, which is one of our local TV stations, was doing [a show about] haunted places of Dayton or something to that effect. They wanted to come in to interview me and Kelly Franz and anyone else who had experienced the energy. They were interviewing me; we were talking about the rustling of the gown and how you can sometimes hear it and so forth. The videographer was standing directly in front of me, and Martha Dunsky, the person who was interviewing me, was standing to my right side. They were maybe 15 or 20 feet [5 or 6 meters] away from me when we were talking about the energy and about the rustling of her taffeta gown."

Although David heard nothing out of the ordinary, he remembered that, at the same moment, both television-station employees "looked over at the 'vom,' one of our stairwells where you get into the balcony. I didn't pay any attention to their stares. I continued to talk. Finally, both of them—the videographer and the person interviewing me—walked over to the 'vom' as if there was something going on, but I hadn't heard anything. They came back and we finished the interview."

Once the taping was finished, David referred to the instance when both the camera operator and the inter-viewer seemed to lose their concentration. "I said, 'What was that all about?' and Martha said, 'Didn't you hear that?' I said, 'Hear what?' "

The interviewer was amazed that David had been oblivious to the strange intrusion during the interview.

"Didn't you actually hear the fabric?" she asked, to which David had to reply, "I didn't." Dunsky went on to describe the sound as being "very soft, as if it was coming into the 'vom' and then, as the sound got up to the balcony, it was very loud. Then it stopped."

David believes that because of the way the three of them had been positioned during the interview process, he'd been too far from the phantom gown's rustling to hear it. "I was quite a ways from it and I didn't hear it, but the videographer said, 'Well, you have a lapel mike on and we had a boom mike going. With those two mikes, if the noise was actually happening we would be able to pick it up.' "

David asked to be kept informed about whether or not the ghostly sounds had successfully been taped.

"About half an hour later, Martha called. She was just ecstatic, practically screaming. I said, 'Can you actually hear it?' She said, 'Yes we've got it on tape. The boom mike picked it up!' "

David continued, "When they aired this show, the hosts were talking about the different places that they had visited and explaining that superimposure had been done in order to give the effect of a ghost. But when they came to the Victoria segment, they said 'What you hear actually happened and we have no explanation for it.' They did get it on tape, so that was really exciting," David acknowledged.

Even today, the spirit of the actress who vanished over 100 years ago is present in Dayton's Victoria Theatre. House manager David Hastings concluded our interview with the assurance that Miss Vicky remains an important and respected component of the theater. "We're real happy that she's here. She's a very positive influence.

When we give tours to children, or to anyone, we let them know that we do have an energy here. It's a positive energy. She's just a friend of the theater."

A soul could hardly ask for a more respectful and welcoming attitude.

SCENE VIII

Dublin's Dandies

The old and venerable Gate Theatre in Dublin, Ireland, has a long and apparently deserved reputation for being haunted. Those associated with the Gate state unequivocally that their ghosts are most "impressive." These claims may be true but no one's come forward with details of the building's haunting, except to indicate that the eerie sounds of phantom footsteps can be heard echoing through areas of the building known to be haunted.

Also located in Dublin is the Olympia, a theater with considerable documentation about its haunted status. Set designer Lona Moran and her experienced assistant, Alf O'Reilly, have had some unexplainable events unfold before them while they were (corporeally speaking) alone in the theater.

One morning in the early 1960s after the couple had been working through the night, they were understandably tired. But neither was able to attribute what they experienced next as a result of over-tiredness. Quite to the contrary, Moran and O'Reilly both felt that, if anything, their senses had been sharpened by sleep deprivation.

The two were in dressing room 9, hoping for a quick meeting over a cup of tea before they each left for their homes. As soon as they settled in, they began to hear a terrible racket—noises that sounded as though someone was rattling a windowpane with great determination. Because they were aware they were alone in the darkened building, they knew that these noises could not have been coming from their own plane in time. They also knew that there were no windows either inside or just outside the dressing room. Neither of them tarried long enough to investigate any further.

Some months later, that same dressing room was vandalized by an unseen presence, presumed to be a poltergeist. The performer who had been assigned to the room admitted that something invisible had been knocking on the door to dressing room 9 every night she'd been there.

Miss Moran had a second experience with a phantom window rattling. This time she'd been standing on the stage and started to walk toward the area where the sound was coming from, but quickly lost her nerve after remembering there was no window at that spot.

Of course that's not to say there never was a window in the Olympia at that location; over the theater's 250 years of existence, dozens and dozens of both recorded and long-forgotten renovations had been done to the place.

Non-existent windows aren't the only components of the old building to make strange and unexpected noises. Doors that still exist have been known to shake and rattle badly when no one's anywhere near them. These eerie incidents can occur whether it's breezy or calm, inside or outside of the building.

Lona Moran, who began her tenure with the Olympia

as a skeptic, has been convinced by the spooky goings-on over the months to change her mind. Stage manager Jeremy Swan's sighting of an inexplicable ball of light might have been an influence in this regard. When Swan came out of a backstage washroom, he felt a presence as he watched a faintly glowing yellow light move at about knee level down the corridor, around a corner and into the haunted dressing room. Worse, this strange anomaly closed the room door virtually in Swan's face! Moments later he stood still and listened in amazement as doors throughout the entire area rattled and banged.

In the late 1950s, a theater electrician named Tom Connor heard footsteps ascending a staircase. Thinking someone wanted to speak with him, he went out to the stairs to meet the other person. No one was there. Puzzled and a bit annoyed, Connor turned on all the lights in the theater so that he could clearly see who else was in the place with him. A sense of a presence and an uncomfortable clammy feeling accompanied the unnerving sounds. Everyone who's heard these footsteps agrees that they are heavy sounds and therefore likely made by a man's feet.

When world-renowned psychic Sybil Leek was brought into the Olympia, she was delighted with all the supernatural activity she found in the place. Leek immediately picked out dressing room 9 as a particularly haunted area but also indicated that the spirits in the theater liked to travel around. She also noted that, in her opinion, not all the souls residing in the theater after death were necessarily connected with the place before death.

Leek identified Dunnevan, a man associated with violence near the Olympia. She gave one example of this phenomenon from 1916. Dunnevan's ghost, the psychic was sure, wanted to leave the theater but did not know how to escape from its confines.

In addition, she also identified a soldier among the ghostly inhabitants of the Dublin playhouse. An accidental killing had occurred in the theater over the Easter Rebellion of 1916, and it's quite possible that ghost is responsible for at least some of the unearthly disturbances.

If the ethereal beings at the Gate Theatre are indeed more intriguing than those in the Olympia, it's a wonder and a shame that they're not more widely publicized than they are. Perhaps those ghosts like to keep to themselves.

SCENE IX

"They Are Legion"

Reg (Dutch) Thompson has worked in one haunted theater since 1977—virtually his entire career. But his association with the building housing the theater goes back even further than that.

Dutch explained the situation to me this way. "The theater is the MacKenzie Theatre in downtown Charlottetown. It's part of the Confederation Centre for the Arts complex, but it's a separate building. The 'MacK' was built in 1929 and opened in 1930 as the Capitol Theatre, a movie house. In the mid-1970s, when Confederation Centre expanded its stage productions to include a second stage, the Capitol was converted to a stage theater."

The location of these theaters is so historic it's amazing they don't have more ghosts. "It's right in downtown

Charlottetown, directly across from Province House, the legislature here and birthplace of Canada, where they held the 1864 meetings [leading to the Canadian Confederation in 1867]. It's probably one of the busiest intersections on the Island," Dutch explained before adding, "Of course, everything's so small here [in Prince Edward Island]."

He continued with more background information. "This second stage, the MacKenzie, formerly the Capitol, is the smaller stage. [The auditorium] holds 200 people. It used to be a cabaret style, but now it's more of a dinner theater. With one exception, the shows [produced here] have been musicals. Where the old movie screen once hung, we have our stage. Directly below that are the dressing rooms, the green room and the rehearsal space. I've been involved with that theater since day one. I work at the theater across the street too, but for the most part—usually between the months of May and October—I'm almost exclusively at the MacKenzie Theatre."

Given this work history, Dutch has had plenty of time to experience the supernatural presence that inhabits the place. Despite such extraordinary experiences, he feels that his encounters with the ghost have been almost *ordinary*, although he does acknowledge that his tenure with the theater has certainly meant that he's "heard all the stories over the years."

"[The ghost stories] are legion. My own experiences are fairly minimal. I'm the lighting designer. I do the lights and am kind of like the crew chief. I look after the scenery and the props and things like that. A couple or three years ago, at intermissions, I would sit in a room

This theater in downtown Charlottetown is understood to be haunted.

behind the lighting booth where my old lighting board is. I would have my radio set up and I would sit and listen to the first 10 minutes of the CBC radio program 'Ideas.' Then I would put a tape in [the radio unit] and would record the last 45 minutes of the show so I could listen to it the next day when I was doing other things. One time, the stage manager, who's also in the same [lighting] booth as me, said to me that people could hear my radio getting gradually louder over in that other room—a room no one else had any access to."

Dutch continued, "This happened a couple of times. One night, I made sure I had the radio turned right down. I had to leave it turned on, otherwise I wasn't able to do my recording. It got very loud. I accused the doorman [of turning the volume up]. He's a friend of mine. I said, 'Look, you should know better. If you're going to play a joke, don't do something like that because it disrupts the show.'"

The doorman, also an experienced theater worker,

"was rather indignant that I even suggest such a thing. He assured me that he hadn't gone upstairs and that no one else went up. He knew this for certain because he's at the lobby for the entire performance. This happened several times and those events are typical of the kinds of things that happened—all very mischievous."

And very ghostly, I couldn't help thinking, as Dutch began to explain another incident that they're sure "Charlie," as they've named the ghost, was responsible for.

As Dutch said, "a variety of actors and musicians" are at the theater during a production. "Sometimes four to eight people will use the green room and the other spaces downstairs. After rehearsals, very often the actors are tired and they don't want to bother going home if there's only a one-hour meal break between rehearsals. I would very often lock them in the building because we have a lot of very valuable equipment in there, and I would leave them [on their own]. If there was ever a fire or something, there were crash bars on the doors [so they could escape the building]. When I've done this in the past, several actors, four or five at least, would come up to me after I'd come back and say, 'I thought you left.' "

Dutch would reply truthfully, "Yes, I went home," to which the actors would retort, "but there were footsteps up on the stage."

Invariably, new theater associates would explain to Dutch that they'd gone up and looked around, but no one was ever there. "The only way to get from the green room and the dressing rooms is to go up the stairs and across the stage. These actors would be lying down on the couches in the green room and they would hear these footsteps. One time, at least two of the people resting heard voices. What they heard was not exactly a commotion, but maybe the sounds of a party. They thought it was the soundman playing with audio tapes."

Those guesses were incorrect because no one but the actors was in the building. "We were all gone. We were all home," Dutch stressed, before adding, "this happened several times."

To avoid adding anxiety to what was already the emotionally charged atmosphere of a live theater, Dutch and the other veteran employees made it a policy never to discuss the ghost with newcomers. No words were ever mentioned about the haunting except, as Dutch described it, "in a form of shorthand. One person would say, 'Charlie's been here recently,' and the other would reply, 'We'll talk about that later.' "

Rather than introduce the supernatural and risk any possible hysteria, Dutch and his cohorts decided that they'd "just wait until we heard any of the [new staff] say anything [about the ghost] over the course of the season."

But it wasn't just the theater staff who were affected by the phantom. Whether as a cabaret or a dinner theater, the building always contained a bar, and the people who worked there were certainly not immune from the ghostly antics Dutch revealed to me.

"Every year, one of the barmaids or one of the actors or one of the musicians or the new stage manager will say, 'I heard the funniest sound and out of the corner of my eye I thought I saw someone walking along [the catwalk].' "

Dutch explained, "These catwalks ring the perimeter of the theater. Everything's completely open. Because of the nature of the building, it was impossible to raise the ceiling [during the renovation from a movie to a stage theatre]."

As Dutch Thompson further warmed to telling the story of "his" haunted theater, his enthusiasm for the place became obvious. "We've had any number of other things happen. I'll tell you about some of those that struck me as being the oddest."

He began. "The MacKenzie Theatre produced a popular musical entitled *A Closer Walk with Patsy Cline*." The runs were highly successful. "We played to sold-out audiences," Dutch recalled. "Over on the left-hand part of the stage, we had built as part of the scenery a sound studio and [a mock-up of a] radio station."

The actor who manned that part of the stage wore clothing of the era being depicted. This included a fedora hat complete with a press pass and a pencil jammed down into the hatband.

"After one of the first shows, [the actor] said, both to me and to the sound man, 'I don't know how you guys are doing that. It's the greatest trick I've ever seen.' "

"What?" Dutch and his colleague asked the actor, who had clearly decided not to be fooled by what he thought was their practical joke.

The man stood his accusatory ground by merely saying, "You know, you know."

Dutch challenged him immediately. "No, really, we don't know."

When pushed for details, the actor explained, "You're somehow pulling the pencil out of my hatband and dropping it on the floor on the stage in front of me just as I'm about to walk on."

His accusation was denied, with justification. "We're not doing that. We're up in the booth at that time."

After that conversation, Dutch realized that the actor, new to the MacKenzie stage, had actually encountered the theater's ghost. "So that's when we told him about Charlie."

The next ghost story from this haunted house was even stranger. Dutch began by explaining the distribution of responsibility between the theater and the adjacent bar. "About 10 years ago was the only time that the bar wasn't run by the Confederation Centre. They had leased out the bar that summer to one of the hotels which ran it with their own staff, their own liquor and their own way of actually selling booze. It was felt that a change of some kind was needed to see if the bar could be more of a moneymaker.

"The new bar operators insisted that all the locks be changed in the bar so that there was only one key that let you into the bar proper, and all the liquor was locked up in a liquor cabinet inside the bar. We always had a master key. There were probably four or five master keys. Only one person had the key that would open both the bar door and the liquor-cabinet door, which was just above the sink in the back room where the food was prepared. That one person was the bar manager, Heather MacKenzie. She had that key on a chain that was around her waist all the time. She was the only one allowed to sign it out and that was the way it was."

While the liquor service was being looked after in a new manner, all the details surrounding the life of the theater and the theatrical workers continued unchanged.

"Over the course of the summer, starting in June, we all brought in our own coffee mugs which we kept downstairs. There would probably have been about 12 of us that summer—this was back in the *Patsy Cline* era. A dozen people but 20 or 24 cups were down there because there were cups that were chipped and broken, just leftovers, and then there were the ones we'd each just brought. Every night the stage manager used to wash them out. We would leave them sitting around, but he was a very neat and tidy kind of person. He would wash them all and leave them on a shelf.

"About a third of the way through the summer, at roughly 7:30 one evening, the stage manager said, 'Look, I don't know what you're doing with your coffee mugs, but we're getting low. We're almost out so please would you go to wherever you have your coffee mugs and bring them in so I can wash them and we'll get back to business.' "

Thinking that he might have absentmindedly left his mug somewhere else in the theater, Dutch checked the places he most usually frequented. "I didn't have any on the lighting board. The audio guy didn't have any on the sound board. The actors didn't have any in their dressing rooms."

A couple of nights passed before the stage manager spoke of the subject again. "I don't see any coffee mugs yet," he chastised those gathered.

Dutch remembered, "We said, 'Well, we don't have any, we don't know where they are.' Within two or three days of all of this, the bar manager, Heather MacKenzie, came to me and said, 'I don't know how you're doing this, but I don't find it funny because I don't have the space. Would you please get your coffee cups out of the liquor lock-up?' Then I looked around through the bar and there, neatly stacked along with the rum and the vodka, were 12 or 15 freshly washed coffee mugs. They were the missing coffee mugs."

Knowing that Heather was the only person with a key for that area, Dutch was not about to accept blame for the antic. He did have an idea, however. "So after the show that night, I got all the bar staff and cast, the orchestra, everybody, together. They were all sitting in the bar having a drink when I said, 'If anyone knows anything about the coffee mugs, could they tell it now, please.' Nobody knew anything. Nothing."

Working in a haunted place apparently requires some unquestioned acceptance from the employees. "So we simply took all those mugs back downstairs. That show ran until nearly November that year, but sometime after Labour Day the same thing happened again. One by one, the mugs disappeared. Heather never said a word. She waited until the mugs reappeared in her liquor lock-up."

Heather still didn't think the situation was at all funny. After all, as the only person with a key to the cabinet, she was responsible for whatever went in and out of there. "She even went so far as to phone her bosses at the hotel and ask, 'Are you people coming in on Sundays or after the shows?' "

No one would admit to such a thing and even today that particular piece of ghostly tomfoolery "is still a mystery."

"That particular stunt stopped, but there are still things that get moved around all the time."

One of the puzzling examples of that phenomenon

affected the stage manager. "The first year he was there, he brought with him a very expensive pair of cowboy boots. Those boots disappeared and he accused everyone of stealing them. Well us easterners don't wear cowboy boots and, besides, they were only a certain size. They wouldn't have fit anyone else."

The boots remained missing all summer. "At the end of the summer, didn't those cowboy boots just reappear on his desk! Now you can never prove that the boots disappearing had anything to do with ghosts, but the way that they disappeared was strange indeed. There were only three of us in the building at that time and I can pretty well vouch for the other people."

Dutch knew that he hadn't taken them himself and he also knew that Charlie liked to play games.

The last of the anecdotes about Charlie that the very patient Dutch Thompson had time to relate was especially convincing to him because it happened during a production in the off-season with no professional actors in the building. This strange incident occurred "12 to 15 years ago," as best the man could remember.

"We were doing *Dracula*. It was in October and the idea was it would spill over onto Halloween. We had all these different people [in the theater], some of whom had never been in the building before. Anyone in the business knows about Charlie the ghost because so many people have talked about him over the years, but a lot of these people [that off-season] were high-school and college students helping out with props and such."

Charlie might have liked all the new faces because, during that time, "there was a rash of sightings. A lot of people heard voices too. It was one of those years when there was a lot of activity with Charlie, for whatever reason. He was more active than normal."

Some of those volunteers, it would seem, got more theatrical experience than they'd counted on.

Other people, particularly Marie, a member of the cleaning staff, began their tenure at the MacKenzie as skeptics, but retired accepting that there was truly something otherworldly going on in that theater.

"Marie used to get very upset with me when I would talk about the ghost. She used to say, 'Dutch, you should be ashamed of yourself. There's obviously no such thing as ghosts and here you are talking about them. I've been here almost as long as you have and I've never seen a ghost.' "

Marie retired without seeing a ghost. She did, however, get a frightening look at what a ghost could do.

For years Marie would work in the theater when there was no one else there. "One night, after she came in early to scold me about telling people of the ghost's presence, she got one of those feelings that she was being watched. She went and checked the doors because she always locked herself in so no one could get into the building.

"Later that night she was mopping the floor in the theater and she looked over. There [within her sight] was a piece of sash cord that had probably fallen off one of the catwalks. It had probably held one of the wires in place, but now it was just lying on the floor. Then," Dutch paused for a breath before continuing his recollection, "it spontaneously lit on fire. Right in front of her. Marie was sure that there was something or someone there. She got the fright of her life!"

Marie fled from the theater and vowed never to return to the place alone. And she never did. The scorch mark, in the shape of a piece of half-inch sash cord, remains in the floor today.

Dutch concluded, "She went from a total non-believer to someone who was afraid to go in the building."

It was quite a profound change of heart. But then, judging by all his ghostly pranks, Charlie's been quite a force to be reckoned with and Marie's not the only employee to swear she'd never be alone in that building again. One evening, Heather MacKenzie and a bartender named Earl were sitting relaxing over a drink after the place was empty and their work was done.

Heather explained to me that the incident that changed her attitude happened "right towards the end of the 1991 season, probably October or November." As she described it, "We were just sitting there and then we heard these voices out in the hallway so we went out, looked around and there was nobody there, but that was quite common. You'd hear these voices. We just came back [into the bar] and sat down again then all of a sudden we heard really loud footsteps going over top of the stage. We didn't even know what was up there. We looked at each other and I'll never forget that. It was as if we were both saying 'Did you hear that?' And these were really loud noises, and we thought that maybe somebody was breaking in there, so we thought we'd better get out. We locked things up very quickly and got out. We ran."

The next day Earl informed Dutch of their experience the night before. Heather remembered that Dutch only smiled and said, "Oh, so you heard the ghost!"

A moment later Dutch asked, "What did the noise sound like?"

Heather informed him, "It sounded like really heavy footsteps going across above the stage but I don't know what it would've been that would have made that sound."

Dutch knew. He stated, "There's a catwalk going across there and the fellow who's haunting the theater was [in life] a workman and he wears work boots."

This explanation fit well with what Earl and Heather had experienced as she stressed, "these were really heavy footsteps."

Although up to that point Heather had not been skeptical, this episode had such an impact on her that she vowed never to be alone in the theater again. Unfortunately, a small incident violated that pledge— but only once.

"I had left a pair of shoes in the theater. I needed them so I went there. I flew in, grabbed my shoes and flew right back out again."

What a good thing Charlie had not decided to hide Heather's shoes! Despite the profound impact the paranormal encounter had on Heather, she staunchly maintains that Charlie himself "isn't scary. He's just a prankster. He has a sense of humor."

From implications made during my conversations with both Dutch and Heather, I was given to understand that the anecdotes they shared with me are only some of the legions of stories about Charlie and the MacKenzie Theatre. Those stories, it seems, are as much accepted as the ghost's existence around the theater. Even his history is known. In the 1940s, a terrible fire broke out on that downtown block of Charlottetown, and it is commonly thought that the then-living Charlie was one of the fire's casualties. Since then, his soul has found its way into the theater. There it's stayed, and for all we know it may stay there forever.

ROYALLY HAUNTED

Ghost Town Ghost

Barkerville, an isolated ghost town in northern British Columbia, claims some of the most unexpected theater ghosts. It was once a booming mining town complete with the pretentiously named Theatre Royal on Main Street. Today most of the town's buildings, including the theater, are reproductions built in 1958 to help turn the dilapidated old town into a modern tourist attraction. Although it's only a replica, the existing theater is reported to be very haunted.

Footsteps are sometimes heard walking across the apparently barren stage. An unrecognizable apparition once joined a chorus line as the dancers hoofed their way across the stage, and performers looking out into the audience will occasionally report seeing another phantom. This most distinctive spirit is resplendent in formal evening wear and sports a nattily trimmed mustache. Whoever he is, or was, the well-dressed ghost is certainly not shy, because many people have seen him.

Even more intriguing are reports of phantom music. Once, while performers took a rehearsal break, they were serenaded over the theater's sound system by dulcimer music, even though the theater's audio facilities were turned off at the time. Surprise turned to shock when the soft sound of a woman's voice began to accompany the lilting tones of the ancient instrument. An extensive search of the premises turned up no plausible source for the impromptu concert broadcast throughout the entire building.

Although it's impossible to know for sure, it would seem that some of the performers from the Theatre Royal's boom years have, since their venue has been reconstructed, returned to recreate their performances into eternity.

SCENE II

The Man in Gray

Theatre Royal on Drury Lane in London, England, is home to a beloved spirit. Although patrons, stage crew, theater staff and others have all been treated to a glimpse of the ethereal character, it's the actors who most welcome a sighting of the ghost known as the Man in Gray. You see, this phantom only makes appearances at shows destined for successful runs.

The ghost's ability to pick hits is uncanny. He was seen walking through the theater during *Oklahoma*, *South Pacific* and *Carousel*, all of which became smash hits. To date, he has never visited the theater when the current play was doomed to end its run prematurely.

Not only does the Man in Gray know how to recognize a hit production, but the spirit of Theatre Royal also knows how to make a fashion statement. He dresses with unmistakable style: high boots, a three-cornered hat on top of a powdered white wig and a gray cloak that only partially hides a decorative (one hopes) sword.

No one has had much luck trying to pin an identity on the Man in Gray. Some say he is the ghost of an actor, possibly either Thomas Hallam or Arnold Woodruffe. Both men were killed in 1735 by Charles Macklin, a fellow actor known for his violent rages. (Macklin's ghost has also been spotted in the theater.) Most people believe the Man in Gray was a member of the theater's audience and not an actor at all.

Whoever he was, the specter is certainly not from modern times, nor even from the 1930s, when some say he first began to appear. A theater has been located at that address on Drury Lane since the middle of the 17th century, but, judging by the apparition's attire, he couldn't be from that era either. His clothing indicates that the man probably breathed his last sometime in the 1800s.

This theory fits with the specter's clothes, the route of his walk and a particularly gruesome anecdote from the theater's history. The Man in Gray always begins his strolls by coming through a brick wall. Not just any brick wall, but the brick wall that workers in the 1850s broke through during a renovation at the theater. That particular piece of demolition wasn't planned, but when workers discerned that the area behind the wall was hollow, they decided to investigate further. They knocked a hole in the wall and discovered a hidden room. The small space had gone unnoticed for years, which is exactly the way at least one person wanted it because, sealed away amid scattered playing cards and coins, lay a skeleton decorated with an accumulation of decades of lacy cobwebs. Although there was no way to determine exactly how long the body had been hidden, the cause of death was still readily apparent: a dagger protruded from between the bones of the body's rib cage.

If the ghost is the murder victim's spirit, then the violence from which he died left no negative imprint on his soul, for he is not a vengeful ghost. As well as being considered an omen of success, his presence has comforted nervous actors through bouts of stage fright.

When actress Doreen Duke was trying out for a role in a play to be produced at the Theatre Royal, it seemed at first that her audition would be doomed by an actor's worst nightmare come true—a totally paralyzing case of stage fright. Duke feared her opportunity would be over before it even began, until she felt an encouraging pat on her back. It was all the assurance she needed to get through the task at hand. The woman won the role with the performance she gave that afternoon, but not before looking behind her to see who'd offered the effective encouragement. It was only then that she realized she had been alone on the stage.

Another actress reported feeling an unseen power propel her around the stage as she performed. She commented later that she felt her performance was greatly improved by allowing herself to respond to that invisible energy source.

The ghost does not always treat the gentlemen in the cast quite so positively. An actor with a most unusual name, Beerholm Tree, reported feeling a definite kick in the seat of his pants as he stood alone on the stage reciting a Shakespearean soliloquy. Perhaps in his corporeal life the ghost was a theater critic.

Unfortunately for potential ghost watchers, there's no way to predict what day the Man in Gray will appear. He might be seen frequently for several days in a row, but then extended periods of time will go by when there are no sightings of his image. When he does appear, it is before nightfall, usually in the afternoons or early evenings. He has never been known to make an appearance after dark, which could lead a person to wonder— can a ghost be afraid of the dark? Possibly so, if his physical body had given up its spirit after being sealed into a darkened room.

Those who have seen the spirit of the theater on Drury Lane agree that his route through the theater is always the same. The illusion begins and ends at the brick wall behind which the skeleton was found, and then it proceeds counter-clockwise via both ascending and descending stairs. When the ghost comes to a plate glass door, he simply walks through without opening it first. His appearances have been witnessed in the middle of matinee performances and even during a bombing raid in World War II. He is silent and bothers no one, nor does he appear to be aware of anyone around him.

Many people who have seen the ghost say that it is like viewing someone from behind a gauze curtain. The image is clear enough, however, that people have given detailed and similar reports of facial features. If anyone approaches the Man in Gray, he simply vanishes.

Audience members frequently testify to seeing the Man in Gray, and occasionally other images, throughout the grand hall. Two women observed a man sitting near them during a performance. Something about the image struck the women as otherworldly and they told a theater employee about it. After poring over the theater's archival records, they came across a photograph of the long-deceased actor Charles Kean and instantly recognized him as the man they'd seen.

Even though he doesn't seem eager to socialize with the living, the ghost is likely not lonely because he has plenty of opportunity at the Theatre Royal to mingle with other entities. Perhaps he chums with whoever, or whatever, moves a particular prop around the theater—an old wooden wheelchair. After being used as a prop for a play, the chair was stored in anticipation of a possible future need. That day has never come, but the wheelchair spends little time in the storage room. It is regularly found in various other parts of the theater with everyone (everyone living, that is) denying responsibility for its movements.

Betty Jo Jones, an actress in the musical *Oklahoma*, maintains she saw the spirit of Joseph Grimaldi, a theatrical clown who died in 1837.

And there have been others. Movie actress Ida Lupino's father, Stanley, a comedian in the early 1900s, was napping in his Theatre Royal dressing room when he woke up feeling that he was no longer alone. Opening his eyes, he saw a shadow move across the room. The image gained solidity and Lupino was able to discern and recognize the form's features. It was the ghost of Dan Leno, a once-famous actor who had died nearly 20 years before.

Lupino may have been in Leno's old dressing room, for the ghost appeared again the next day to both Stanley Lupino and his wife. Mrs. Lupino didn't take the ghost's appearance as calmly as her husband did. Instead, she fainted dead away.

Actor Tony Britton holds bragging rights to the most disturbing ghost story connected with this theater. Before a performance of *No No Nanette*, Britton was alone in his dressing room when he was suddenly thrown to the floor. Something both strong and invisible had pulled his chair out from under him. That same evening, many people backstage watched and listened as an invisible presence played a typical ghostly game by turning every radio in the building on and off while no one was near any of them.

The Man in Gray and the other ghosts are in no danger of being chased from their home turf. The theater's management is very accepting of its haunted status and even goes so far as to point out the different "haunts" during scheduled public tours of the building. It seems they feel the Theatre Royal on Drury Lane would not quite be itself without its collection of resident ghosts.

SCENE III

Caspar and Others Encounter a Ghost

The Theatre Royal in southwest England's resort community of Margate survives in splendor and, in all likelihood, with its ghost. Considering the changes this theater, the second oldest in Britain, has been through, both facts offer testimony to the power of tenacity.

The theater in Margate is like at least three other English theaters: it is haunted by the ghost of a woman wearing gray. But in this instance, there is a difference because this ghost's identity is presumed to be known. The phantom is widely accepted as being the spirit of actress Sarah Thorne, who ran an extremely successful theater-based school of acting in Margate from 1874 until her death in 1899.

In life, Sarah Thorne strongly believed in the premise "the show must go on" and even on her deathbed she declared that she would never leave the theater she loved. From reports throughout the 20th century, it would seem that the woman's spirit has kept her word.

In the spring of 1934, skeptic Caspar Middleton took over running the haunted Margate. Within the first weeks of his association with the place, Middleton had witnessed the apparition three times, a serious threat to his naive skepticism! These sightings were so clear that he was able to describe the route the specter took (which included passing through a brick wall where Thorne's work area had once been) and the manifestation's attire. It seemed to him that the ghost wore what the actress had been wearing when she performed the sleepwalking scene as Lady Macbeth.

Several months after those sightings, actress Peggy Ford-Carrington was rehearsing at the Margate for the opening night of a play called *The Naughty Lady*. She later recalled being startled by the sound of a moan emanating from one of the box seats. She looked up and saw an image leaning over the railing and frantically waving its arms. Not surprisingly, Ford-Carrington cried out in shock and terror. Her screams brought another actress out onto the stage. The second woman saw the illusion briefly before fainting.

Seconds later, Caspar Middleton rushed to the stage to see what all the fuss was about. He too saw the ghost and he immediately ran to that seating area. It was empty and there were no signs to indicate that anyone had just been there. Ford-Carrington, meanwhile, had not immediately lost sight of the image. She had watched transfixed as the ghost defied gravity by floating toward the roof, where it disappeared.

When news of the sightings became public, Sarah Thorne's niece came forward to advise that, as long ago as the 1890s, her aunt had spoken of the theater being haunted by an entity wearing a gray habit. That additional information served to create some confusion as to the identity of the ghost, but phantom noises and even indistinct sightings of strange, inexplicable shapes continued until the theater was closed during World War II.

Upon the reopening in July 1948, supernatural phenomena in the theater at first picked up where they had left off and then they increased in frequency. Lights that had been turned off were turned on by an invisible hand. Locked doors were found unbolted. More than a dozen people heard the sound of phantom cries followed by footfalls proceeding across an empty stage. A tiny glowing ball of orange light cut a path across the stage. As it did, the eerie manifestation, which made its way along a never-changing trajectory, grew in size until it was as large as a soccer ball, before disappearing toward a stage door.

In the early 1960s, when the theater was used as a bingo hall, the ghostly activity apparently ceased. The next witnessed supernatural event came in January 1966, when a painter named Alfred Tanner worked alone in the theater for two nights. His enigmatic encounters were reported in a local newspaper after Tanner explained to a journalist that he had heard doors slam as well as sounds of people whispering and coughing in the empty theater.

By the time the painter had also seen the heavy stage curtain slowly lift up and a woman's head and neck appear, he had taken all he could of working alone in the haunted theater. The next night he brought a friend, Lawrence Rodgers, along for company. Performing to an audience of two, instead of just one, did not deter the ghost, who proceeded to cause "a terrific crash, as if something very heavy had been thrown from the balcony." The men ran upstairs to see if they could catch the culprit, "but could find nothing," according to Rodgers.

At that point, Tanner went home while Rodgers went to the police, who then sent a search party to scour the theater. Nothing was found, but the ensuing publicity served to reawaken interest in the mystery. As a result, two men, James Chell and Thomas Redshaw, both with an interest in the unexplained, kept an overnight vigil at the Margate. They too heard phantom noises, some that they described as sounding "as though several large pieces of furniture were being dragged about," others as crashes. Even after careful investigation, no source for these noises was found.

The pair did find that at 1:30 AM the theater became "intensely cold." Lights went on and off when there was no one (visible) near any of the switches, pockets of strange smells developed spontaneously and then mysteriously dissipated, and the noises continued—including the sounds of a nonexistent clock ticking and "shufflings and scratchings."

It wasn't until the third occurrence—when Chell and Redshaw saw "a dirty brown patch" appear on a wall that had been built after a set of box seats had been torn out— that they decided it was time to leave the theater.

By then, the time was 4:30 AM. A curious constable on patrol noted their hasty departure from the theater, and he asked them where they were coming from and why they were on the street at that hour. Their answers were especially interesting to the officer: the police had received, just minutes before, a call from a resident of a house near the theater. The caller had reported hearing the sound of an explosion coming from the theater but the officers who investigated found the place empty and undisturbed.

Given the haunted history throughout this Margate entertainment hall, the ghost story is clearly more complex than people once thought it was. Perhaps Sarah Thorne's spirit does reside there, but it would seem unlikely that she is there alone behind the heavy curtain of time.

SCENE IV

Other Gray Ladies

An empty theater is somehow an inherently eerie place. Perhaps that was why a sighting of the ghostly Gray Lady at the Theatre Royal in Northamptonshire, England, was always especially unnerving. This resident revenant never gave off any indications of malevolence. She just floated throughout the century-old building after the audience and cast had left for the day.

On a dark and gloomy night, T. Osborne Robinson, a theater employee for 50 years, had a dramatic encounter with the phantom. As he and a co-worker finished some chores backstage, they heard footsteps echoing from an area of the theater that should have been empty. The pair called out, asking who was there and what the person wanted. When their questions went unanswered, the men left their work to investigate. It was then that they saw the apparition of an old woman clad in gray. Amazement turned to horror as the ghost moved toward them before walking directly *through* Mr. Robinson on her way out of the building.

"I was rooted to the spot with fear," Robinson declared later.

The Gray Lady has also been seen by actors as they perform on stage. Her image is clear enough that the witnesses were able to report details of her appearance— including that she was dressed in a hooded cloak. Others have not seen her, but instead are adamant that they have felt her presence.

Although he is now retired, Theatre Royal employee Bryan Douglas saw the ghost on three separate occasions when he served as the theater's front of the house manager. Twice Douglas saw a person entering a workshop. Thinking that someone was trespassing, Douglas followed. The only way out of the room the image had been seen entering would have required walking right past Douglas, which no one did. Yet both times when he reached the room, he found it empty.

Douglas' third sighting occurred early one evening when he had stepped outside the building to put something into his car. From the parking lot, he watched a person cross the street and approach the theater's stage door. Because it was twilight, Douglas expected that, when the person opened the door, light from inside the building would shine through the doorway. When this didn't happen, Douglas hurried to the stage door. He reached his destination just in time to witness the form of a woman, dressed in a gray hooded cloak, walk through the closed door.

All of these sightings took place before renovations

were done to the theater in 1984. These alterations included removing an old tombstone, which had been rather unceremoniously used for many years as a doorstop. Since the ghost stopped appearing immediately after that, it has long been assumed that her spirit was somehow associated with the grave marker.

The Theatre Royal in Northamptonshire is not entirely free of paranormal phenomena. People associated with the place still speak of feeling a sudden inexplicable chill or having the distinct sense of a presence being with them even when there is supposedly no one else in the room.

• • •

Ghostly gray ladies are also in residence at the Theatre Royal in York, England, as well as in Bath, England. The former is said to be the ghost of a nun who was still alive when she was mercilessly bricked into a wall of the convent that once stood on the theater's lot. The latter ghost is thought to be connected to the male ghost seen in the Garrick's Head Hotel next door. The story goes that the couple's deaths took place in the 1700s and that a love triangle was implicated. The man's ghost is more active, but the theater ghost has been seen frequently enough that she is known for her gray-colored dress.

The Empress Theatre

The very haunted Empress Theatre in Fort Macleod, Alberta, is old only by western Canadian standards, having held its premiere in 1912 after two years of construction. Judging by an effusive report in the *Lethbridge Daily Herald*, which included phrases such as "a first-class theatre…[having] every modern accessory…[and] a great addition to the appearance of the town's chief thoroughfare," the finished venue was considered at the time to have been well worth the wait.

There have been many changes at the Empress in the intervening years. Thanks to the concerted efforts of many citizens, the theater remains every bit as great an addition to the town today as it was when "Texas Tony and his Wonder Horse Baby Doll, accompanied by the Purple Sage Riders" strutted their way across the stage. One noteworthy change that history seems to have wrought upon the theater is that it is now home to a ghost.

Dozens of people have experienced the phantom presence and their reports are amazingly consistent. Everyone is sure that there is only one presence in the building and that the spirit is a man who was not a performer but rather was involved in the business end of the theater.

Juran Greene, former manager at the Empress, is a big man with a warm handshake and a booming deep voice. Juran is also a confident man, not someone given to flights of fancy or unnecessary nervousness. He spoke with calm assuredness about the spirit housed at the Empress Theatre.

Whether it's by the ghost of Dan or Ed, this western Canadian theater is certainly haunted.

The ghost was not a constant presence, Greene explained, but when it was around, "it always let me know." In typical ghostly fashion, the unseen resident liked to play with the lights in and around the theater. Even when he was alone in the building, Greene would find that banks of lights, which he knew were turned off, had suddenly become illuminated.

Actor Bruce Watson, who played the venue, described feeling "a cold spot at the front of the house." He also reported having "a strange feeling [that] someone was standing over my left shoulder down the back stage staircase. I mean, I really felt like there was someone there."

The ghost at the Empress has actually been seen by several people. An actor reported that he was momentarily distracted by the sight of what was clearly a ghost. That apparition exactly matched the descriptions from both a theater employee and a patron, each of whom spoke of seeing an image "with big, hairy arms, wearing a brown shirt."

Patrons have purchased tickets from "an elderly gentleman," even though the theater was entirely staffed by women on those occasions. The manager of one production acknowledged that, night after night during the run of his play, he had seen the same ghostly image sitting in the same balcony seat.

There is great debate as to the ghost's identity. Some think it's the spirit of longtime owner and manager Dan Boyle, who bought the Empress in 1937. Others think the ghost is Ed, a former caretaker at the theater. Diana Seboerg, a member of the society now running the theater, believes the latter and she's had several encounters with the resident ghost.

"I've heard him walking in the theater and the alarm goes off lots," she began. "He's also tapped on the projection booth window."

The ghostly stunt that most unnerved Diana, however, occurred when she and another woman walked into the theater. "Joyce was humming a tune," she recalled. "When she stopped, Ed whistled its ending."

Whoever the ghost might be, he certainly can be a prankster. The seats in the theater are spring loaded to fold up out of the way when they are not occupied. Sometimes Ed or Dan will put on quite a spectacle for the people closing the theater after a show, making the seat bottoms go up and down seemingly of their own accord. When he isn't busy playing his own silent version of musical chairs, the entity likes to make a nuisance of himself by throwing garbage out of the garbage cans where staff members had just placed it.

Another time, a group of employees gathered together

for a break from work. They watched in collective awe as a coffee cup moved around a table. Thinking that the bottom of the cup was wet, someone picked it up to wipe any such friction-reducing moisture away. The tactic might actually have worked, except that both the cup and even the table on which it had rested were dry. When put back down, the cup moved again.

Former Empress Theatre employee Trent Moroz noted that the feeling of the presence had been "especially strong after [showing certain] films." He said that sometimes, when he was locking up, he could "feel a cold breath from the theater itself."

Surely only a thoroughly haunted building could evoke such a description.

SCENE VI

The Most Beautiful

Hyperbole abounds in descriptions of theaters. A survey of the literature about these "palaces of the night" nets at least two different theaters purported to be "the biggest," "the grandest" or "the most expensive" theater ever. No comparisons with other theaters, it is implied, are necessary or even possible. While all of this bravado might render even the most devoted theater-lover cynical, it seems widely accepted that the Haymarket Theatre Royal in London, England, is at least *one* of the "most beautiful" theaters in the world. And it is just as widely accepted that it is haunted.

The ghost has been identified as John Buckstone, who managed the theater from 1853 to 1878. In 1861, he saved the theater from almost certain financial demise by hosting a new production—*Our American Cousin*—the same play that, four years later and thousands of miles away, was being performed at Ford's Theatre in Washington, D.C., the evening that John Wilkes Booth assassinated President Abraham Lincoln.

Mr. Buckstone's concern for the Haymarket did not cease with his physical death. He's been nearly as active at the theater since his death as he was during his life. Although the man died in 1879, his image has been seen frequently throughout the 20th century. Sometimes the apparition would merely sit in a box seat. During the run of the colorful play *Hadrian VII*, it is suspected that the former manager paid a call to the seamstress, who responded to a knock at her workroom door by telling the visitor to "come in and sit down." She was no doubt expecting that her caller would be one of the actors needing a costume adjustment. She was most surprised, therefore, to see a man wearing distinctly Victorian-style clothing. When she questioned the image, he smiled at her and then simply vanished. The woman recognized the specter as that of John Buckstone.

Staff occupying the office area that was once set aside for Buckstone's private use quickly become used to the sounds of phantom footfalls as well as the sight of a door opening and closing when no one is near it.

In 1967, when a potential train strike threatened to grind movement within the city of London to a halt, renowned actress Dame Margaret Rutherford, who was performing a role in a Haymarket production, decided to stay the night in the theater. Although she no doubt did not enjoy her sleepless night, she was pleased to report that she had seen the ghost of John Buckstone. She felt that the sighting was a good omen for the success of her current play.

For a time shortly after his death in the 1920s, Oscar Wilde's ghost joined Buckstone's in actively haunting the theater.

It seems that the Haymarket Theatre Royal is not only a truly beautiful theater but also a truly haunted one.

SCENE VII

Ghosts Galore

Showbusiness magazine once referred to Toronto, Ontario's Royal Alexandra Theatre as "the most beautiful on the North American continent." This assessment is no doubt somewhat subjective, but the theater is certainly among the most splendid and lavish to be found anywhere, and it is definitely one of the most haunted.

The Royal Alex's stage has hosted the best entertainers and entertainment the world has known. From 1913 until the early 1940s the legendary Al Jolson occasionally performed there. In 1997 the Alex put on the show *Jolson*, a tribute to the entertainer's life. During the entire run an eerie blue light floated above a particular balcony. During one scene, an actor opened a hatch leading to the orchestra pit. There, dressed in old-fashioned clothing, sat the specter of a man. Moments after the actor saw it, the image vanished and the unnerved thespian had to continue his role as best he was able, pretending that his extraordinary encounter had not occurred. Perhaps the phantom image was Jolson himself.

The ghosts at this beautifully refurbished theater are welcome patrons.

That apparition is only one of many ghosts in the well-haunted Royal Alex. The existence of these specters is so accepted that, when recently asked about the ghosts, publicity and promotions spokesman Randy Alldread replied by forwarding a copy of an extensive article on the subject from a recent edition of *The Globe and Mail*, a usually staid Canadian newspaper.

Not surprising for a venue that has, over its long history, welcomed as many people through its doors as the Alex has, there have been deaths both in the building and connected with the theater. Some of these deaths might account for its current gaggle of ghosts.

One of the presences remaining in the theater is believed to be the spirit of a former "flyman." The person in this demanding occupation is generally situated in the fly gallery, high above the stage, to operate a complex series of ropes that descend from the gallery and are attached to equipment and scenery on the stage.

On Halloween 1994, Darrin Carter, the lighting man for the show *Crazy For You*, was in the fly gallery when he watched as a headless specter walked past him at his isolated post far above the stage. The sighting was so distinct that Carter was able to describe the apparition's clothes.

The phantom flyman cannot be lonely in his hereafter, because there are numerous spirits in the Royal Alexandra Theatre to keep him company. Many people claim they can still feel the presence of a patron who died in her second balcony seat while enjoying a production at the theater.

Employee Luis Rebelo is occasionally required to be alone in the Royal Alex overnight. The ghost stories surrounding the grand old dame of King Street West never fazed Rebelo, because he was a determined skeptic. And he kept that attitude—until his first encounter with the ghosts in the theater, coincidentally, as he worked his first-ever graveyard shift. The incident occurred just after he had checked the building thoroughly and knew it to be empty.

Initially, when Rebelo heard sounds of conversations coming from the dressing room area, he wondered which of the actors had unaccountably remained and he decided to phone through to each of the dressing room extensions until he got an answer. Not one of Rebelo's calls was answered and yet he continued to hear the sorts of sounds that one associates with being at a party. He was even able to pick out a bit of what was being said, including the phrase, "Yes, yes, we'll have to do this again."

Wanting to capture some physical proof of his paranormal experience, Luis Rebelo sprinkled powder on the floor around the dressing room area and then left. Later, when he heard doors swinging open which he knew he had locked, he went to investigate more thoroughly. There were footprints scattered through the powder he'd spread.

Since that first encounter with the phantom voices, the auditory scene has replayed itself frequently enough that Rebelo now accepts the ghosts' presence. He even thinks that another entity may have been added to the roster—Vic Egglestone, a man he once worked closely with. The two had devised a code, a rhythm on the door buzzer, to alert each other when they wanted to come into the theater after hours.

Not long after that routine was established, Egglestone passed away after a long illness. Rebelo is sure that the man's spirit remains in the theater, because on several occasions he has heard the buzzer sound the distinctive and secret pattern he and Egglestone had developed. Each time that has happened, Rebelo found there was no one at the door. No one he could see, that is.

The chair in the office that once belonged to Egglestone is a most ordinary chair, even though it has occasionally acted in a most extraordinary way. Rebelo has gone into the office, seen the chair in the middle of the room and attempted to move it to the side. The small, standard-issue steno chair refused to budge. No matter how hard Luis Rebelo has pushed it, he could not make Egglestone's old chair move even slightly.

Despite the strangeness of that situation, Rebelo could not have been entirely surprised by it, for he has often sensed his former co-worker's presence in that small office. Occasionally when he goes into the deceased man's office, it will have that extraordinary chill in it that has come to be associated with the presence of a ghost.

Whether they were former stage actors, backstage technicians, office staff or former patrons, ghosts from the past along with present employees and patrons continue to share in their enjoyment of this "most beautiful" entertainment palace.

SCENE VIII

Palace Players

Ehrich Weisz is not exactly a household name and yet even today, more than 75 years after his death, people all over the world still marvel at his feats of magic. The reason for this apparent contradiction is that the magician astounded audiences with his amazing tricks of deception only after having adopted the stage name of "Harry Houdini." Although he died many years ago, in 1926 at the age of 52, Houdini's mastery of his craft is still held in high esteem.

Beatrice, his widow, anticipated that her late husband would send her a sign that he had successfully passed over to the great beyond. In January 1929, the grieving woman signed an affidavit declaring that she had finally received a message from him. Shortly after that, she retracted her claim, saying that she could not be sure it had been her husband's ghost who had communicated with her.

The woman never again spoke with any assurance on the subject, and many people speculated that it was Beatrice's declared doubts that prohibited Harry Houdini's soul from finding eternal rest. His apparition was seen at an estate near Hollywood, California, and is also believed to have visited the Palace Theater in New York City when that venue was hosting a musical based on Houdini's life.

Initial preparations for the show were little short of a nightmare. Nothing, apparently, went well. In addition to the challenge of finding an actor skilled enough to perform the complex leading role, the director also had problems with other cast members and even with the financiers backing the show. In frustration, those in charge of the production turned to a Ouija board and through it asked the spirits for assistance. The board's pointer spelled out a rather mysterious message—"I'll send a sign."

Satisfied with the response, the group started back to work, this time with a decided sense of optimism. Something within the atmosphere of the project had changed. Everyone began to work more happily and with greater cooperation among them.

When rehearsals were finished and it was almost opening day, a decision was made to decorate the outside of the theater with strips of silver foil. No sooner had the ribbons been hung than a gust of wind blew up (literally out of a clear blue sky) and whisked the strips of foil into the shape of the letter "H."

On opening night, the same letter was found painted on a prop—the trunk used to help re-enact many of Houdini's escapes. All corporeal beings with access to the theater were questioned. Each one denied responsibility for the strange act.

Harry Houdini's positive spirit may have been required to overcome a pre-existing spirit in the theater. During the 1950s, Louis Borsalino, a member of the

tightrope act *The Four Casting Pearls*, fell while performing at the Palace. Seriously injured, he was rushed to the
hospital but died a short while later. That tragic event
seemed to have affected the theater's atmosphere. Actors
peering through the stage curtain before the audience
gained admittance reported seeing and hearing a man
walking across a rope above the stage, losing his balance
and screaming as he fell. Witnesses took such a sight—or
even just hearing the long-deceased acrobat's screams—as
a bad portent. Harry Houdini's ghost saw to it that such
horror and subsequent fears were overridden at least
sufficiently so that the story of his own life could successfully be played out for the public.

Thousands of miles away, another theater named the
Palace is also reputed to be home to a ghost. The grand
old theater in London, England's Cambridge Circus
opened in 1891. The ghost of legendary ballerina Anna
Pavlova is thought, by some, to have created chaos in a
locked dressing room while the man assigned to the area
was on stage performing. Pavlova's spirit apparently came
through during a séance and informed participants that
she threw the man's belongings about in anger, and that
she, having once been jilted by a former lover, would hate
all men—for all eternity.

Another specter said to have haunted the Palace in
London was that of former actor Ivor Novello. His ghost
was seen on several occasions shortly after his physical
death in 1951. For the most part, that image never disturbed
anyone, but in 1980 auditions held at the Palace for a play to
be staged at the Theatre Royal on Drury Lane (see "The
Man in Gray," page 170) were interrupted by an actor who

was distracted by someone moving about in one of the balconies. As a small group of amazed people stood on the stage staring at the apparition, a runner went up to escort the trespasser out of the theater. By the time the man reached the place where the image had been seen, the area was empty. The ghost had disappeared. Descriptions of the manifestation led people to believe that a former manager—a man who had been dead for many years by that time—had at least momentarily returned to check out what was new in his former workplace.

Perhaps any palace, even a theater called the Palace, is too wonderful a place for anyone's soul to want to leave.

SCENE IX

Ghostly Confluence

Actors are, almost by their very nature, superstitious folk. Colleagues never wish one another well before a performance by saying "good luck," but rather utter the seemingly incongruous phrase "break a leg." Another part of theater lore maintains it is very bad luck to whistle in a theater. But the worst theater faux pas that anyone involved with a particular Shakespearean production can make is to speak the name of that play. Actors, producers, set designers or anyone with any sort of a role to play in the performance will simply refer to "The Scottish Play." This ritual is viewed as a sensible way to avoid causing havoc, and possibly otherwise unexplainable injuries, among the members of the company producing the great drama.

In this retelling of the ghost story, "The Scottish Play" will be referred to by the name the great playwright gave his work: *Macbeth*. It is generally accepted that a murder described in *Macbeth* took place in Glamis Castle, near Perth, Scotland. The building originally served as a hunting lodge and is the Bowes Lyon family's ancestral home.

Some researchers feel that it is highly unlikely that the *actual* murder took place in the castle, because the dates simply don't make sense. The murder was to have occurred in the 11th century, fully 300 years before the main part of the castle was constructed. Despite this historical discrepancy, the play—fraught with ghostly activity—and the very haunted castle have become permanently and inexorably linked in people's minds.

There can be no doubt that both the building and the play have supernatural elements. Glamis Castle, where the Queen Mother was born and where she, in turn, gave birth to Princess Margaret, is widely believed to be haunted. One of the suits of armor lining a castle corridor is said to be possessed by a spirit. He's proven that he's not a shy individual. Tourists will occasionally report that they have inadvertently taken the ghost's photograph.

Although the spirit in the suit of armor, presumably a knight, lived in a very different era from the ghost of the Gray Lady, another phantom who haunts Glamis, it would appear that he has something of a paranormal crush on the ghostly Gray Lady. His armor is often found lying by the door to the area where the lady's apparently alluring spirit is thought to reside.

Can there be any wonder that a play about a ghost, supposedly set in a haunted castle, has an undying connection to our theatrical ghost legends?

Jake: At His Majesty's Service

It is difficult enough to interpret a living human being's actions and motivations, so it is probably complete folly to think we can understand spectral gestures. Keeping this caution in mind, it is still interesting to wonder if the phantom residing in His Majesty's Theatre in Aberdeen, Scotland, might have something of a sense of humor, for his ghostly presence is usually perceived in one of the eeriest parts of the old building. Fortunately the spirit's identity is known, and "Jake" is considered a friend to the theater and to all of those people associated with it.

His Majesty's Theatre opened on December 3, 1906, but it did not become haunted until a tragic accident occurred during World War II. During those war years, cities in the British Isles were often under nighttime attack and all lights had to be extinguished or windows covered at night with blackout curtains. Without these precautions the cities could have become clearly marked targets for the enemy's bombers. Nighttime entertainment normally held outside, therefore, was either cancelled or moved indoors. In 1942, when the circus came to Aberdeen, performances were held inside His Majesty's Theatre.

Animals were hoisted, one at a time, to and from the stage via a platform operated by an ingenious system of lifts and pulleys. Once, for unrecorded reasons, someone led two horses onto the device. It was a fatal mistake. The combined weight of the animals put too much stress on the ropes and stagehand John (or "Jake," as he was more commonly known) Murray was decapitated in the terrible crash that resulted.

Ever since, staff members have reported feeling, and even hearing, Jake's presence. Generally he walks about on a staircase leading from the basement to the uppermost seating area. Although the sudden realization that one is accompanied by an invisible presence has certainly startled some witnesses, Jake is absolutely accepted as a positive and protective influence in the theater. In return, everyone associated with His Majesty's Theatre is equally positive about, and protective of, their resident ghost.

Whether Jake's spirit loiters about the spooky staircase out of a sense of fun or whether the staircase is spooky because a ghost is there is really the only enigma in this otherwise well-understood Scottish ghost story.

GRAND GHOSTS
& PHANTOMS *of the*
OPERA HOUSES

Grandly Haunted

Legend has it that the Grand Street Theater in Helena, Montana, is home to an enduring and benevolent spirit. Clara Bicknell Hodgin was the wife of a Unitarian church minister and died in 1905 at the tender age of 34. She loved children and had been both a classroom and a Sunday School teacher. One of the unique ways she chose to instill lessons in her students' minds and hearts was to involve them in stage plays.

After Clara died, the congregation demonstrated their grief over her death and their appreciation for her dynamic life by having a beautiful stained-glass window commissioned for the church. Some 15 years later, when the church moved to another location, the building became a library and the artistic glass memorial was placed in storage. By "coincidence," more than 40 years later the stained-glass window was discovered, undamaged, just weeks after the Grand Street Theater company took over the Unitarian church building.

Almost as soon as theatrical productions, which Clara had so loved, and the congregation's artistic tribute to her were brought together in the church, the haunting became an accepted fact in the stately old place. Phantom footsteps are reportedly heard echoing throughout an otherwise empty building. The sounds routinely follow a specific route, coming in the front door and climbing the stairs before going into the main part of the building. Although staff have become used to the noise patterns,

during renovations before the theater opened one workman admitted to being badly shaken by hearing someone
climb a staircase—a staircase that had been removed.

On another occasion, a witness reported watching in
awe as a light, so white it seemed to be tinged with blue,
made its way down the stairs. A theater patron also
claimed to have seen the image and described a female
face superimposed on a haze of light drifting up near the
ceiling. More commonly, the specter manifests herself
simply as a feeling of a presence, or as pranks and movements throughout the building.

Two women who were working alone in an area under
the stage were frightened to hear the sounds of someone
walking directly above them. Worried that someone had
broken into the building, they ran to see if they could
catch the intruder. No one was there. There was no one
else anywhere in the place, nor had there been, for the
locks were still securely in place. Nevertheless, the two
knew that they'd heard someone walking across the stage.
They soon came to the conclusion that the spirit of Clara
Bicknell Hodgin was with them as they worked.

Like most ghosts, the guardian of the Grand enjoys
playing with electricity. She causes lights to dim and
flicker or come on and go off when there's no mechanical
reason they should. Once she turned on both the lights
and a radio in a work area.

Clara's ghost has even demonstrated that her love of a
practical joke has survived into the afterlife. When an
employee was trying to get organized to leave the theater
after a production one night, she was thwarted at every
turn. Carrying props that had to be removed from the

theater, the woman switched off all the lights. Once she'd left the area, she glanced back only to see the lights were turned on. Thinking she hadn't hit the switch firmly enough, she laid down her awkward load, went back into the room and flipped the switch again. No sooner had she picked up the props again than the lights were shining once more. Thinking that a fellow employee was hiding in the theater and playing a trick on her, the woman turned the lights off again and called out in annoyance that she'd had enough of the joke and was already late to pick up her little boy. After she heard a peal of feminine laughter coming from the balcony, the curtain across the stage billowed and the lights came on again. There was no way anyone—well, no one of this world—could have been responsible for all those activities at the same time.

The next morning, perhaps hoping to reassure herself that she hadn't been alone with a paranormal being the night before, the woman confronted the person she presumed had been behind the series of pranks. The accused looked completely dumbfounded and assured her colleague that she'd been nowhere near the theater after closing.

It would be interesting to know whether Clara Bicknell Hodgin was a tidy person in life because her ghost certainly seems to be. So tidy, in fact, that she can become very annoying to members of the theater's production team. On one occasion, props that had been put out onto the stage because they were needed there were continually removed and put away again. All this mysterious activity was accompanied by the sounds of floorboards creaking where no one could be seen.

Few people are as superstitious as those involved in show business. Almost every theater has what they call a "ghost light"—a single bulb that is left turned on, ostensibly to provide at least some illumination for the first person into the building but, more whimsically, for the ghosts in the building. At the Grand Street Theater, the "ghost light" has been seen to glow brightly at times when it is not even plugged in.

Despite the undeniable strength of the haunting at the Grand Street Theater, once people get used to the presence they are no longer frightened by it. By now, those interested in stage plays, both the living and the long-deceased, exist harmoniously in at least one location in Montana's capital city.

SCENE II

Exit Dying

The story of the Grand Opera House in Oshkosh, Wisconsin, dates back to the 1770s. Through the years, many credible people have told tales of spooky experiences in the auditorium, but it wasn't until the 1970s, when a group of university students used the Grand to film a movie about a haunted theater, that the place was really recognized as having a resident spirit. As a result, the ghost story surrounding the Opera House is layered, a little like a set of stacking Russian dolls or the optical illusions created by the opposing mirrors of a circus funhouse.

The movie the students produced was *Exit Dying.* Actor Henry Darrow played the lead role of an aging entrepreneur involved in purchasing rundown theaters and renovating them before selling them again for a profit. Although the character's renovation projects had been successful in other cities, nothing was going smoothly for him in this particular fictionalized town.

At first, Darrow's character is captivated (and temporarily thrown off focus) by a beautiful woman involved with the town's amateur theater troupe—a group that didn't approve of the man's plans for the playhouse. Once that complication is overcome, an evil politician tries to undercut his plans. Eventually the movie's plot reveals that behind all the "bad luck" lies the malevolent presence of the theater's resident ghost. By the final scene, good triumphs over evil and the businessman/renovator ends up with the theater and the girl. There's just enough plotline for a made-for-television movie, which is good because that's exactly what this project was.

Such a movie needed to be filmed in a theater, so the haunted Grand Opera House in Oshkosh was chosen. By coincidence, like the theater it was to represent, the Grand was also being renovated at that time. Owner Bill Seaton was willing to have his property used for the movie, but the film crew had to work around the Grand's scheduled performances. This meant that the movie was filmed at some very odd hours—usually from midnight to 7 AM— the graveyard shift, so to speak.

By the time the film was "in the can," the actors all had a few ghost stories to add to their repertoire of life experiences and some had even had firsthand encounters with the ghost. An actor named Larry Schroeder was the first to suspect that he'd had direct contact with the phantom. Schroeder's part called for him to remain suspended from a perch high above the stage for nearly an hour. As soon as the scene was finished, stagehands lowered Schroeder to safety. No sooner did the man's feet touch the stage than the rope that had held his weight all that time suddenly broke. It was the first time anyone involved had ever seen a rope breaking *after* the weight it had been bearing was removed. Many who witnessed the bizarre occurrence immediately credited the ghost of Percy Keene, who had been the stage manager at the Grand from 1795 to 1865.

When the movie crew presented their theory to owner Seaton, he wasn't surprised and told them, "I was up on the balcony about 3 AM. All the doors…were locked and I know I was the only one there. I heard footsteps coming up the stairs." Seaton turned around to see who had gained entrance to the locked theater, but no one was there—that he could see. "I stood with my mouth hanging open, the footsteps came right across the balcony and stopped dead in front of me!"

Suddenly the importance of the work he'd been doing decreased considerably in Bill Seaton's mind and he left the theater. "That's the last time I ever worked there alone at night."

During the filming of *Exit Dying*, two grips (theater handymen) experienced the type of fright Bill Seaton must have felt that night. The men were doing what grips often do—waiting to be needed—when they had an experience neither man would soon forget. They sat and watched as "someone walked out of the orchestra pit and through this little door into what used to be the lower level box seat."

Both men knew all the members of the current project's cast and crew, but they didn't recognize this individual.

They were extremely apprehensive and they watched the doorway the man had gone through, waiting for him to come back out and identify himself. He never did.

"We must've watched that door for five minutes and no one came out. [W]e decided to go over and see what was going on," grip John Jansen recalled.

Together, armed with a flashlight to illuminate their way, the two opened the door they'd seen the man enter through just minutes before. "I don't need to tell you that we were surprised to find no one. This little room [the box seat] couldn't be more than 15 feet square [about 5 meters] with only one door. There just wasn't any way that anybody could have gone out of there without our seeing him. We both saw this character go in and we both know that he didn't come out."

And yet the apparition was nowhere to be seen. The enclosed area was empty. Both men reported the experience to their co-workers and two young women were able to offer genuine empathy. They too had been through a frightening ordeal. Theirs took place in the basement of the building where a labyrinth of tunnels runs under not only the theater but also good-sized sections of the Wisconsin city.

They were nervous, but not unnerved, during their subterranean tour, until they came to an area that suddenly felt extremely cold. They stood stock still and stared at a form on the dirt floor in front of them.

"It looked like an oil slick on water but it was…shining with its own light. It began to rise up…and took on something like a human shape only without legs. It stuck an arm out toward us like it was going to touch us. We both screamed and it just melted back down into the dirt."

The terrified women cut their explorations short and ran for the comforting company of their co-workers. They couldn't have been completely surprised by the incident, though, because one of them had already suffered through an unexplained encounter in the basement tunnels. She had been walking with half a dozen others when she felt a hand grab her ankle so tightly that it held her, paralyzed in place.

Undaunted by making a film about a haunted theater in a haunted theater and sharing otherworldly experiences, the crew and cast of *Exit Dying* decided to probe even further into the realm of the unexplained. They plotted and staged as controlled an experiment as they could in order to objectively document the theater's abnormal presences.

The entire company locked themselves into the auditorium and silently waited. The resident ghost certainly did not try their collective patience. Less than five minutes after assembling, the group watched as a "shadowy, human-like shape" made its way slowly, from left to right, across the stage. The sighting disappeared into an area leading to one of the theater's side doors. Seconds later, the door was heard to open, and those gathered watched as reflected light from the street bathed the stage area with an eerie glow. A moment later, the door closed, leaving the stage dark once again.

Despite all the distracting and sidetracking intrusions—both corporeal and ethereal—*Exit Dying* was successfully filmed. Soon after, the cast and crew gathered to celebrate by enjoying the first-ever showing of the movie. The opinions after the viewing were unanimous. The film had turned out well, even better than they'd hoped it would. Better still, it would seem that *they* weren't the only ones pleased with the finished product. The phantom of the Grand Opera House, who was seen viewing the screening from a balcony, apparently smiled down benevolently on the assembled filmmakers.

Producer Bob Jacobs recalled the ghostly sighting this way: "I could see him clearly. His face was round, cherubic, friendly. He wore glasses and his gray hair was close cut, behind a high receding hairline. His eyes twinkled—there was no mistaking him for a shadow...I watched him for about 30 seconds before the projector shut down and everything went black."

The projectionists also caught a glimpse of the specter and immediately yelled for someone to turn some lights on so they could see more clearly. In the few seconds it took to carry out their request, the ghost had vanished.

Some of the braver company members went up to the balcony. There was no one there, but the seat where the ghost had been spotted sitting was the only seat folded down in the entire balcony. Every other seat bottom was folded up against the back of its chair as would be expected in an empty theater. The apparition, which closely matched the description of deceased stage manager Percy Keene, was gone. He had, however, left those involved in *Exit Dying* with a tangible memento of his presence. As is standard in movie making, the crew took many still photographs throughout the weeks of production. One of those photos included a strange "smoke-like swirl at the edge of the negative. Next to the swirl is a dark figure [with its] head and shoulders visible..."

The photographers checked both the negative and the section of wall on which the image appeared. "There was nothing there to account for it on the negative [and] I can tell you that it is not a stain on the wall," reported Bob Jacobs.

Schroeder and colleagues were not the first to be affected by Keene's influence, for members of little theater groups using the venue had frequently reported feeling a presence in the place. Because the spirit seemed to watch over them and protect them, the amateur actors had always presumed that the ghost was the soul of the long-serving stage manager.

During their tenure in the theater, the spooked actors began to compare stories with others who had used the Grand. Amateur theater companies using the place had dozens of unaccountable reports. Actors had felt they were being watched when there was no one (visible) nearby. Others had witnessed doors opening and then slamming closed in vacant areas of the auditorium.

One member of a group calling itself Drama Lab had a truly remarkable experience during a performance. He was rushing from his dressing room to wait for his cue. He hurried around a corner approaching the stage and nearly bumped into a man wearing clothes that would have been in fashion in the late 1700s. The image carried a program for a play entitled *The Bohemian Girl*. That play had run at the Grand in 1795, the first year of Percy Keene's 70-year-long corporeal tenure with the place.

It would appear that even death hasn't been able to end the stage manager's loyalty to and enjoyment of the theater he loved.

A Grand Ghost

The history of London, Ontario's Grand Theatre virtually demands that it be haunted. And it doesn't disappoint.

Theater magnate Ambrose Small was proud of all the theaters he owned, but this one, on Richmond Street, was his absolute favorite. It took everyone by surprise when Small mysteriously vanished from Toronto in December 1919. His body has never been found but his spirit has inhabited the beautiful old building in London, Ontario, from that day forward. During a séance held when the theater was dark, a spirit voice counseled that "the secret to Ambrose's death lives in the west wall." Needless to say, that area of the theater has been carefully preserved, but it has not yet been explored.

The first ghost sighting of Ambrose at the Grand may have been just shortly after the man was last seen alive, many miles away, in Toronto. A night watchman on duty that evening swore that he both saw and talked to the impresario's image. The employee's claim was taken seriously enough that the entire building was searched—in vain.

Former Grand manager and confirmed skeptic Paul Eck remembers looking into the balcony area of the theater and seeing a "distinct shadow" for which he could find no cause. When he worked alone late at night in the theater, it wasn't tiredness or work overload that would occasionally send him home earlier than he'd planned. It was the stress of knowing that he was locked in an empty building,

The ghost of this theater's former owner is still in the "house."

yet listening to phantom footfalls on stairways and watching lights turn off by themselves.

The night that actress Charmion King was the last to leave the building she stood, momentarily frozen in awe, as a strange and apparently sourceless light "walked" along an elevated catwalk.

The ghost of Ambrose Small is always treated with respect at the Grand, although his presence can sometimes be something of a nuisance. He has appeared in actors' dressing rooms and also caused problems during performances. During the run of *Anne of Green Gables*, Small's ghost was blamed for the sounds of phantom footsteps that were heard in the balcony, as well as for the sand that mysteriously poured from the fly floor during a rehearsal.

More recently, his image was seen by an actress while she was on stage. The sight of an apparition floating in a reclining position, as though suspended above the heads of the unsuspecting audience, must have given the poor woman's stage composure quite a jolt.

In typical ghost-like fashion, Ambrose's spirit has caused electrical appliances to act in peculiar ways. During the last season before massive renovations got underway, a camera malfunctioned and, for reasons no one was ever able to identify, the film that had been loaded into it was ruined. More recently, a hissing sound for which no source could ever be found vibrated throughout the "haunted house."

Ambrose is also presumed to have been the person who opened the production booth door and peered in while a play was in progress. As soon as the producer acknowledged the face, it disappeared. She later described the ghost's appearance as a white face with dark hair—a description that, according to old photos, could easily have applied to Ambrose.

But Ambrose Small's ghost is not the only one in the theater. An apparition of a woman, believed to be that of a former cleaning woman, has been sighted on the theater's stairs. And when the Grand hosted a production of the James Reaney play about the Black Donnellys of nearby Lucan, Ontario, the entire clan of Donnellys, or their manifestations anyway, left their usual homestead haunt and joined the cast and crew in London.

And so the legacy of the ghost-filled Grand Theatre in London, Ontario, continues to surround the staff members who love the haunted old place so dearly.

Phantom of the Opera House

The Muskoka district in the province of Ontario has long been internationally renowned for its geographical splendor. Increasingly, over the past quarter of a century, it has also become known for palatial vacation homes that dot the shores of the beautiful lakes in the area. Gravenhurst, a small town at the south end of Lake Muskoka, is home to the Gravenhurst Opera House and Arts Centre—the Op, as it is affectionately known to its patrons.

The building has been a landmark for nearly a century, but there is little about today's Opera House that is recognizable from the floundering theater structure it was just a few years ago. Thanks to a huge expenditure of time, money and effort, the hall is once again as impressive as it was originally. It is also haunted.

The phantom of the Op is thought to be that of Ben, a former lighting technician who fell to his death while working in the theater. Ben's presence is generally cited as the cause when doors slam closed unexpectedly or a draft or a spot of cold manifests itself in an otherwise still, warm area. As with many ghosts, Ben likes to tinker with things electrical and has been known to turn lights on and off when no one else is near them.

Lee Madden, a volunteer at the theater, told a reporter with the local newspaper *The Muskokan* that she had once heard phantom footsteps, followed by the sound of a door slamming. Lee also spoke of an even closer encounter, possibly with Ben. She suspects that the ghost laid his hand on her shoulder. Taking the tactile connection with the supernatural presence amazingly calmly, Lee informed the ghost that she was very busy and therefore needed to be left alone to continue her work. The spirit apparently obliged.

Considering that renovations often either provoke resident ghosts into further activity or into leaving a place, it's reassuring to find that the more things change at the Gravenhurst Opera House and Arts Centre, the more they also seem to be remaining the same.

SCENE V

Always Elvira

A beautiful ghost in an elegant opera house in an almost Norman Rockwellesque quaint town—what more could a person with glamorous, ghostly interests ask for? As a ghost hunter, perhaps official acknowledgment of the gorgeous, ghostly Elvira would be high on the wish list.

That recognition does not seem to be forthcoming, however. Woodstock Opera House employee Jan Link indicated to Jo-Anne Christensen, author of *Ghost Stories of Illinois*, that the tale is deemed by the theater's administration to be fiction. "Folklore, all the way," according to Link. As a result, we must satisfy ourselves with the widespread and longstanding acceptance of the ghost in Illinois' Woodstock Opera House.

Many well-known show business people, including Paul Newman, Orson Welles, Shelley Berman, Tom Bosley and Geraldine Page, have worked at the Opera House— and not just on the stage. Berman was working alongside the set crew putting the finishing touches on scenery when he first became suspicious that the Opera House was home to a ghost.

The comedian was quoted as saying that he had witnessed spring-loaded seats in the auditorium lowering as if some invisible presence had just sat down. Once, he watched in amazement as a party of five—presumably a ghostly party of five—silently sat down in a row of apparently empty chairs. As all good culture vultures would, those spirits knew enough to be quiet while they were seated but between shows phantom sounds were often heard.

Berman, among others, also recalled hearing disembodied footsteps coming from parts of the building that were known to be empty at the time. And many people involved with the theater have admitted feeling a presence when no one (visible) was near them. Perhaps that eerie sensation led to the general feeling that the building "creaked too much," Shelley Berman acknowledged before adding the disclaimer, "the word 'ghost' was used sparingly."

Oddly, "spirit" seemed to be the more acceptable word for the ethereal presence said to be residing at the Woodstock Opera House. Perhaps that is why she has come to be called Elvira, in honor of the spectral character in Noel Coward's play *Blythe Spirit*.

Even though she is not officially acknowledged, Elvira the ghost is well known throughout not just Woodstock but McHenry County. She is thought to have been an actress at the Opera House during the 1790s, the theater's very earliest days. Scuttlebutt has it that, after an unsuccessful audition, she killed herself. Some say she jumped from the building's tower to the sidewalk below, and others are sure she hanged herself. Since then, on occasion, she's been seen in seat DD113. Other times the spring-loaded base of that seat has been seen lying flat when there is no one (visible) in it. The long-dead actress has been known to call out critical comments at rehearsals, and during performances if Elvira is unhappy with a show, she's said to cause the lights in the Opera House to flicker and eerie echoes to reverberate throughout the auditorium.

A rather gruesome version of this ghost story has Elvira managing to inflict her own suicidal thoughts upon the minds of young actresses. Fortunately all the women so affected have managed to overcome her murderous ghostly intentions before they actually jumped from the tower.

On a more pleasant note, Elvira has actually been seen by a credible witness: a member of the Opera House's board of directors. She was seen as a "beautiful" woman with "golden hair cascading to below her slim waist," wearing an attractive ball gown.

In addition, Gina Belt, a community resident, swears that an invisible hand helped her to readjust a feather boa that had slipped from her shoulder.

While no one immediately associated with the elegant old performance hall was willing to attest to the haunting on a broadcast of NBC's *Today Show*, Elvira's image is so well established that it was used during one of the first extra-special commercials prepared for presentation during a Super Bowl broadcast. The ad began with the Woodstock Opera House's executive director, Eva Bornstein, accompanied by her dog, getting ready to leave work for the day. As she does, she apparently fails to notice that a theater seat, which had been down, folds upward, as though some invisible presence had just stood up. This scene was followed by the door to the lobby opening and closing, apparently of its own volition, and the dog looking back at something. Then the animal and its owner, who is still unaware of any unusual activity, climb into their car (a Honda) and drive away. The voice-over indicates that Eva Bornstein believes in Hondas, not ghosts.

So while staff at the Woodstock Opera House may not officially acknowledge its status as a haunted "house," they're not opposed to a bit of profitable joking about Elvira's presence. Maybe that's a fair trade, because it means the ghost is able to enjoy her luxurious surroundings without fear of being chased away by a pesky exorcism.

Majestic Mysterious Manifestations

According to John Lindsey's book, *Palaces of the Night*, The Majestic Theatre in San Antonio, Texas, "was one of the biggest and grandest [theaters] ever built." There can be little doubt that his description is accurate. The 4200-seat auditorium opened in 1929, and the grand opening was reported to have been a gala event attended by celebrities from around the globe. In addition to its larger-than-average size, the Majestic is remarkable for its exquisite and thoughtful design. The Spanish-castle style, complete with faux windows looking out onto gardens, is topped by a perfect evening sky. This artistic creation was designed not only to make the patrons feel as though they had been transported to a nearly magical land, but also to counteract, at least visually, the sweltering heat patrons may have suffered through during a typical San Antonio summer's day.

The ghosts at the Majestic are not constant presences but rather phantoms that come and go frequently enough to give staff members or other workers an occasional fright. Dee Rodriguez explained that although she is no longer associated with the theater, she was one of the house managers during the 1970s. By coincidence, the man who later became her husband owns the company that now cleans the theater. As a result, Dee Rodriguez is very familiar with all facets of the large and splendid auditorium.

She began our interview by explaining, "I don't know if [the theater] is '*haunted* haunted.' First of all, places that hold that many people are normally electrified by the end of a show and so you have lots of noises and lots of creaking and lots of 'stuff' after the people have left."

But she willingly acknowledged that the goings-on at the Majestic can go beyond what Dee clearly felt were normal, expected reactions from a building just emptied of a large group of people with all their chemistries, electricities and emotions.

"These aren't hairy-scary stories, but there *are* things that happen in that theater."

Dee continued, "There's an area that used to be the Majestic offices. It's called the 'tunnel.' In the tunnel, you can hear clanking [sounds] even though there's no machinery down there that actually works. You *can* hear clanking. You can walk by there on certain evenings and the clanking will be really low, but there are other times when the clanking is really loud."

No explanation has ever been found for this strange phenomenon.

In describing the one possibly supernatural event that occurred to Dee, she prefaced her retelling by stating, "I don't know if it was my imagination."

Whether the event was internally or externally manifested, it was certainly memorable.

"I was on the third-floor balcony one time, checking the [cleaning] crew's work. I was going from the men's restroom to the ladies' restroom when I could have sworn I heard somebody call me by my real name, which is Dahlia. Hardly anybody knows that name, just family and people who have known me for a long time. In the theater most everybody calls me 'Dee.' "

That night she "was walking right by the stairs that lead up to the balcony and somebody said 'Dahlia.' I thought it was my husband because he would be one of the only ones to call me by that name. I turned and I looked. Nobody was there."

Puzzled, Dee went looking for her husband to confirm what she hoped was true—that he had called her name. She asked, "Were you up there in the balcony? Did you call me?"

Dee's husband Pepe informed her flat out, "I haven't been up in the balcony for a long time."

She paused for just a second before ending the story with an indication that the incident still puzzles her. "It was just one of those things, I guess."

In addition to all those other memorable encounters that are not easily explained, a very matter-of-fact event occurred that will also never leave Dee's mind.

"A while back, 1974 or 1975, when I was one of the house managers...a patron...died in the theater right before a performance. The man who used to be the stage manager/technical director and I had to move the deceased gentleman from his seat and place him into another area of the theater until the ambulance came. Of course we knew he was dead but nobody else did at the time."

Dee continued, "My husband wasn't involved in the theater at the time of that death. We were not even dating. The event was something [my husband] heard about much later."

Despite this chronological qualification, Dee was quick to acknowledge that, if anyone was going to see a strange presence in the Majestic, it might well be her husband Pepe or a member of his janitorial service staff. "They're the ones who run around there at midnight and three o'clock in the morning."

By the time the following incident occurred, Pepe and Dee were married, and he had heard the story about his wife having to carry a corpse out of the auditorium.

"One day, my husband told me that they were cleaning inside [the seating area of the theater] and that he saw a gentleman standing at the back, near one of the doors, looking at him. [Pepe] turned around and was going to ask 'May I help you?' but, by the time he could get the words out, the door had closed and the gentleman was gone."

This incident definitely piqued Pepe's interest in his wife's experience from years before.

"What did the man who died look like?" Dee recalls him asking her. "I said, 'Well, he was a tall gentleman.' "

Pepe asked, "Was he white-haired?"

Dee confirmed that, yes, the patron who died in his seat had white hair.

Pepe continued to probe. "Was he wearing a gray suit, a white shirt and a red tie?"

Dee was shocked when her husband added those details. "There's no possible way he could have known that. Not at all."

Dee's husband then went on to describe, in more detail, the image he'd seen. "He just stood there. He was staring at me until he made me turn."

Once observed, the image of the long-deceased patron vanished.

And that's not the only male apparition who's been

seen in the haunted house. Dee remembered a time when the cleaning staff "were working in the dressing room area. One of the ladies that Pepe had in his crew started screaming about a blond-haired guy being in the dressing room area. The crew started looking in all of the dressing rooms. They started chasing [around] to see if they could catch anything or anybody."

No one, nor any thing, was ever found, but "the woman who'd seen the manifestation kept saying that there was a blond-haired man present."

Dee concluded that this was another example of a mystery at the theater. "Who this one is, I don't know. He had been standing in the hallway in the dressing room area. Just standing there. [The woman who saw the presence] immediately called my husband and the next minute [the ghost] was gone. The cleaners checked all entrances. All the doors were locked from the outside. Nothing ever came of that. It was just a single sighting."

BIBLIOGRAPHY

Belyk, Robert C. *Ghosts: True Stories from British Columbia.*
Ganges, British Columbia: Horsdal & Schubart, 1990.

Christensen, Jo-Anne. *Ghost Stories of British Columbia.*
Toronto: Hounslow Press, 1996.

Coleman, Loren. *Curious Encounters, Phantom Trains, Spooky
Spots, and other Mysterious Wonders.* Boston: Faber and
Faber, 1985.

Colombo, John Robert. *Haunted Toronto.* Toronto: Hounslow
Press, 1996.
———. *Mysterious Canada.* Toronto: Doubleday, 1988.

Huggett, Richard. *The Curse of Macbeth.*
———. *Supernatural on Stage.* New York: Taplinger, 1975.

Hurwood, Bernhardt J. (Ed.) *The Second Occult Review Reader.*
New York: Award Books, 1969.

Jackson, Robert. *Ghosts.* New York: Smithmark, 1992.

Lamont-Brown, Raymond. *Phantoms of the Theatre.* New York:
E.P. Dutton, 1977.

Lindsey, John. *Palaces of the Night: Canada's Grand Theatres.*
Toronto: Lynx Images Inc., 1999.

Myers, Arthur. *Ghosts of the Rich and Famous.* Chicago:
Contemporary Books, 1988.
———. *The Ghostly Register.* Chicago: Contemporary Books,
1986.

O'Donnell, Elliott. *Scottish Ghosts.* Norwich, England: Jarrold & Sons Ltd., 1975.

Olsheski, Constance, Mike Filey and John Lindsey. *Pantages Theatre: Rebirth of a Landmark.* Toronto: Key Porter Books, 1989.

Reaney, James. *The Donnellys: A Trilogy.* Victoria, British Columbia: Press Porcepic, 1983.

Simmons, James. "Leadville's Tabor Opera House." *Historic Traveler,* July/August 1995.

Skelton, Robin and Jean Kozocari. *A Gathering of Ghosts.* Saskatoon, Saskatchewan: Western Producer Prairie Books, 1989.

Smith, Suzy. *Prominent American Ghosts.* New York: Dell, 1967.

Spencer, John and Anne Spencer. *The Encyclopedia of Ghosts and Spirits.* Volume 2. London, England: Headline Book Publishing, 2001.

Vath, Richard. "Theater Ghosts." *FATE* Magazine, September 2000.

Winer, Richard and Nancy Osborn. *More Haunted Houses.* Toronto: Bantam Books, 1981.

～

GHOST
HOUSE

Ghost House Books

Look for these volumes in our popular ghost story series:

Canadian Ghost Stories	1-55105-302-0
Even More Ghost Stories of Alberta	1-55105-323-3
Ghost Stories of California	1-55105-237-7
Ghost Stories of Hollywood	1-55105-241-5
Ghost Stories of Texas	1-55105-330-6
Ghost Stories of the Rocky Mountains	1-55105-165-6
Ghosts, Werewolves, Witches and Vampires	1-55105-333-0
More Ghost Stories of Saskatchewan	1-55105-276-8
Ontario Ghost Stories, Vol. I	1-55105-203-2

Coming soon...

Watch for these upcoming volumes from Ghost House Books:

Campfire Ghost Stories	1-894877-02-0
Ghost Stories of Indiana	1-894877-06-3
Ghost Stories of Michigan	1-894877-05-5
Ghost Stories of the Maritimes, Vol. II	1-894877-01-2
A Haunted Country Christmas	1-894877-15-2
Haunted Hotels	1-894877-03-9
Ontario Ghost Stories, Vol. II	1-894877-14-4

Available from your local bookseller.

For more information, contact our customer service department. In the
United States, call 1-800-518-3541. In Canada, call 1-800-661-9017.